THE ENCYCLOPEDIA OF
MUSICAL INSTRUMENTS

NON-WESTERN
& OBSOLETE
INSTRUMENTS

Produced by Carlton Books Limited

20 Mortimer Street

London, W1N 7RD

Text and Design copyright © Carlton Books Limited 2001

First published in hardback edition in 2001 by Chelsea House Publishers, a subsidiary of
Haights Cross Communications. Printed and bound in Dubai.

First Printing

1 3 5 7 9 8 6 4 2

The Chelsea House World Wide Web address is http://www.chelseahouse.com

Library of Congress Cataloging-in-Publication Data applied for

Woodwind and Brass Instruments ISBN: 0-7910-6091-8

Stringed Instruments ISBN: 0-7910-6092-6

Percussion and Electronic Instruments ISBN: 0-7910-6093-4

Keyboard Instruments and Ensembles ISBN: 0-7910-6094-2

Non-Western and Obsolete Instruments ISBN: 0-7910-6095-0

THE ENCYCLOPEDIA OF
MUSICAL INSTRUMENTS

NON-WESTERN
& OBSOLETE
INSTRUMENTS

ROBERT DEARLING

Chelsea House Publishers

Philadelphia

THE ENCYCLOPEDIA OF
MUSICAL INSTRUMENTS

NON-WESTERN
& OBSOLETE
INSTRUMENTS

Woodwind and Brass Instruments

Stringed Instruments

Percussion and Electronic Instruments

Keyboard Instruments and Ensembles

CONTENTS

Non-Western and Obsolete Instruments

We saw in the Introduction how instruments were discovered accidentally and haphazardly. Some developed rapidly and their use spread widely among primitive peoples; others evolved slowly as if awaiting later technological developments, new materials and advanced workmanship. The main beneficiary of the sophisticated mechanical devices that have made advances in instrument-making possible has been Western music, though some other cultures have pursued their own developments to often extraordinarily elaborate lengths. Consider, for instance, the complicated stringed instruments of India compared with the basic examples of Tibet.

In less-developed cultures, musical instruments have evolved only modestly from basic designs thousands of years old. They did not need to change: they fulfilled the requirements asked of them, and more pressing needs were found for the often meagre resources available to early man; changing perfectly adequate instruments just for the sake of it was not a priority. Development was not important; diversity was.

'Blow', 'scrape', 'pluck' and 'bang', the four original methods of producing sound from instruments, continue to hold good, but designs are constantly changing in literally hundreds of ways. While a drum, for instance, still retains the original components of membrane and resonating body, different designs have multiplied so vastly that their number is no longer quantifiable. And what applies to 'bang' applies equally to 'blow', 'scrape' and 'pluck'. Only a small fraction of the different types that belong in each of these categories can be dealt with here, but that fraction is large enough, one hopes, to indicate the amazing diversity of instruments to be found in Africa, the Middle East, the Orient and Asia.

Also included here are some ancient instruments that have been obsolete for so long that, by existing in a different era, they have become just as 'foreign' to us as those instruments from non-Western cultures. This seems doubly appropriate if one considers that religious considerations of great antiquity often play a more fundamental role in non-Western than in Western musical activity. As Longfellow wrote:

"These are ancient ethnic revels/of a faith long since forsaken."

The standard Western grouping into woodwind, brass, strings and percussion cannot cope with every possible type of instrument, so in this section of the book we have used less formal divisions. That said, even 'blow', 'scrape', 'pluck' and 'bang' cannot account for every example! We will begin this survey by looking at blown instruments.

Although dates are given where known (or surmised from available evidence), it is not possible to attempt a chronology. Musical archaeology has not progressed far enough for even guesses to be advisable in most cases, but it is safe to assume that many of these instruments are older than existing evidence leads us to believe. Alphabetical ordering, then, has been chosen instead of anything more scientific.

PRIMITIVE MAN IMPROVISED HIS INSTRUMENTS FROM WHATEVER MATERIALS WERE TO HAND. BY DRILLING A MOUTH HOLE IN A DISCARDED ANIMAL HORN A USEFUL SIGNALLING INSTRUMENT WAS CREATED (FAR LEFT). THE HUNTER'S BOW (TOP) WOULD PRODUCE A NATURAL 'TWANG' WHICH WAS AMPLIFIED WHEN A GOURD WAS ATTACHED TO THE WILLOW WOOD. MODIFIED GOURDS (MIDDLE) WERE USED AS DRUMS AND RATTLES. A FEW STRIPS OF THIN METAL FASTENED TO A SUPPORTING BOARD WILL VIBRATE WHEN DEPRESSED AND RELEASED BY FINGERS AND THUMBS. THIS IS THE 'THUMB PIANO' (LEFT).

𝄞 BLOWN INSTRUMENTS

THE PRINCIPLE ADOPTED by the player of a 'blown' instrument is simple: air is forced down a tube. However, unless some way is found of modifying that passage of air, all that will emerge at the far end is air, its sound perhaps slightly changed by the hollowness of the tube. Various means of making that modification have evolved.

𝄞 AN *ALPHORN* (OR *ALPENHORN*), TYPICAL OF THE TYPE USED IN EUROPEAN MOUNTAIN REGIONS FOR SIGNALLING.

In the recorder and flute the air strikes a sharp edge which makes it vibrate, while in other instruments (eg, clarinet and oboe respectively) one or two reeds in the mouthpiece vibrate and impart that vibration to the air. Alternatively, the player's lips create the vibration, as in the trumpet and horn, where specially shaped mouthpieces assist in controlling the vibration.

Once the column of air is set in vibration, a note will be produced. This note may be altered by perforations along the length of the tube which are opened or closed selectively by fingers, or by keys or valves operated by the fingers. The timbre of the note may be changed according to whether the tube is cylindrical or conical. In most cases the air is directed along the tube straight from the mouth; an exception is the bagpipe family, in which a reservoir of air in a bag is introduced into the pipe by pressure, the reservoir being replenished as necessary by the player's breath through another pipe. Another exception is when the air in a flexible reservoir is driven past tuned valves by the pressure of the hands, as in a concertina or bible organ. In these cases the air is replenished through inlet valves. In larger organs, bellows, either manually or mechanically driven, supply the air. Other exceptions will be noted as they arise.

𝄞 Alphorn

Most famous for its signalling role among the peaks of the Alps, the first reference to an *alphorn* dates from the 15th century, though the instru-

ment is certainly much older, probably prehistoric. A hollow tree trunk once provided the basic material, and wood remains its source of construction. The player stands at one end, the instrument stretching away in front of him, its upturned far end resting on the ground or on a stand. The sound, resembling that of a cow in agony, echoes over great distances. Some alphorns are so long that the time it takes for the sound to emerge can be measured. Peter Wutherich, a resident of Idaho, built an *alphorn* in 1984. It is 24m (78.7 feet) long; its sound travels that distance in 73.01 milliseconds.

𝄇 Anata

Two possibilities, both Peruvian. The *anata* is a primitive wooden flute with a mouthpiece; the name also refers to a species of panpipe with half-a-dozen canes.

𝄇 Aulos

This double-reed instrument may still be heard in Mediterranean folk gatherings, its piercing tone dominating the ensemble. It dates from the ancient Greeks. The Romans called it *tibia*. It is no accident that their word for the instrument means both 'flute' and 'shin-bone' – the latter often provided the material for the former. The lung pressure

𝄞 A WOODEN FLUTE OF PERU, THE *ANATA*, EMBELLISHED WITH GOLD ORNAMENTATION.

COMPONENTS OF THE
Bagpipe
%

THE BAG: The skin of a lamb or goat, sealed airtight. This acts as an air reservoir. The player squeezes the bag (under the arm, between the knees, between arm and chest, etc) to feed a continuous supply of air to the chanter and drones.

THE BLOWPIPE/BELLOWS: The blowpipe is a reeded, sometimes double-reeded, pipe through which the player blows air into the bag via a non-return valve. Some designs use a bellows depressed by hand or knees to supply the air.

THE CHANTER: A pipe with fingerholes (and, very occasionally, keys) which the player uses to produce the melody. Some designs have a double chanter, either in one block or separately: the second may be either a second melody pipe or a drone. Chanters usually terminate in a small bell, but animal horns of various sizes have been encountered.

THE DRONES: Reed pipes exiting the bag and usually sounding continuously while the instrument is being played. Three drones are common, two and one less so. Some designs dispense with a drone altogether, in which case the instrument is little more than a reed pipe with a bag which provides a continuous flow of air .

required to make the aulos sound is phenomenal; players once bandaged their cheeks to prevent them from splitting. Perhaps to allow more air to escape, two- and three-pipe *auloi* developed, affording the melody pipe a drone accompaniment. Greek virtuoso *aulos* players were extravagantly feted as they travelled from town to town bedecked in jewels and clothes of amazing colours and quality. Crowds gathered to hear them, and the players would, for a handsome fee, condescend to give lessons to the better-off.

% *Bagpipe*

The bagpipe was invented, probably by a shepherd with spare animal skins and bones to hand, somewhere in the East, c. 5000 BC. Reports that it arose in China cannot be substantiated. An area covering India and extending westwards to Syria is likely, the most probable location being Sumeria, where at this time many basic devices, including wheeled vehicles and the plough, were invented.

♪ AN ADAPTATION OF THE ANCIENT
BAGPIPE-MAKER'S ART: A SCOTTISH
BAGPIPE WITH MOUTHPIECE,
CHANTER AND THREE DRONES.

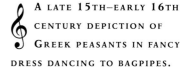

♪ A LATE 15TH–EARLY 16TH
CENTURY DEPICTION OF
GREEK PEASANTS IN FANCY
DRESS DANCING TO BAGPIPES.

In the early Christian era the bagpipe spread eastwards as a folk instrument, into India and west and north into eastern Europe. By the Middle Ages it was well established throughout this area and even into western parts of Europe.

European courts accepted the bagpipe as a 'respectable' instrument in the 17th century, at the same time as countless different designs of bagpipe were evolving in folk circles. By the 18th century, though, the bagpipe was in decline everywhere except in the Balkans and the extreme west and north of Europe.

The Americas, Australia, Africa and the East beyond India have no traceable bagpipe culture apart from local groups of enthusiasts. Even in India, if bagpipes are heard today they have usually been made to Scottish designs.

Bagpipes

COUNTRY BY COUNTRY

In the following geographical plan we begin in the Middle East, as did the bagpipe, and move gradually westwards. The similarities in names reveal interesting connections between instruments, and suggest lines of evolution not otherwise obvious. All these bagpipes are mouth-blown, except where bellows are mentioned.

IRAQ: *zummara bi-soan*, a short blowpipe with a large goatskin bag, two parallel chanters in a block with separate bells, but no drones.

PAKISTAN: *bin*, a gourd bag, two parallel pipes, one a chanter, the other a drone, played by snake-charmers. *Mashq*, a simple blowpipe-to-bag-to-chanter and a single drone. Similar instruments are found in northern India (*moshug*) and Hindustan (*masak*).

BELORUSSIA: *duda*, various simple forms of the Czech *dudy*.

ROMANIA: *cimpoi*, similar to the Hungarian *duda* but made in five different designs.

BULGARIA: *gaida* or *gayda*, a generic term for 'bagpipe', found in Macedonia, the former Yugoslavia and Greece, where the commonest bagpipe (*tsambouna*) has a single chanter and single drone. *Dzhura*, a high-pitched instrument in eastern Bulgaria; its low-pitched counterpart is called *kaba*.

SLOVAKIA: *gajdy* and *gajde*, a small version of the Bohemian *dudy*.

SERBIA AND FORMER YUGOSLAVIA: *gajde*, a bellows-blown low-pitched bagpipe with an oval chanter containing two channels. There is a large, upturned wooden bell. The Albanian *gajde* is similar. *Dude*, bellows- or mouth-blown, with a triple chanter.

POLAND: the *koza*, distinct from the Ukrainian *koza*, has a three-channel chanter, one being a drone, and two additional drones. The chanter has no bell. *Koziot*, like the Czech *dudy*, was originally mouth-blown when introduced in the 14th century but now has bellows. There is a single chanter and a single drone. The *koziot* is often played at wedding ceremonies.

GREECE: *askaulos*, an ancient Greek generic name for the bagpipe. Today it is called *zampouna* (*tsambouna* in the Greek islands): a droneless bagpipe whose double chanter terminates in a small, sharply-upturned bell. Far to the west, in the Balearic Islands, Greek influence is felt in the *zampona*, a shepherd pipe in which the two drones can be silenced.

HUNGARY: *duda*, with a double chanter in one rectangular block of wood.

BOHEMIA/CZECHOSLOVAKIA: *dudy*, a bellows-blown but originally (14th century) mouth-blown, instrument with curved chanter and a curved single drone, each terminating in a large bell. The outlet to the chanter may be carved in the shape of a goat's head. Similar instruments are found in Belorussia and, called *hoza*, in the Ukraine, while in Germany *dudy* refers to a small pipe.

GERMANY: *Sachphîfe*, *Blâterfîfe*, are ancient generic terms of today's *Schäferpfeife* ('shepherd pipe') and *Platterspiel* ('bladder-play'), and *Dudelsack* is derived from Balkan names. The *Hümmelchen*, a small pipe, has long since vanished, and the *Bock* is now obsolete. Introduced before 1600, the *Bock* had an elongated chanter that terminated in a large horn curving out at right-angles.

ITALY: in Ancient Rome *tibia* was both shin-bone and flute; *utarius* was a person who carried water, often in an animal skin, and the *tibia utricularis* was the 'flute-skin', or 'pipe-bag'. By the 16th century the name had become *zampogna*, from the Greek, and had come to refer to two different instruments. The first type has two separate chanters and is played mainly by street musicians for dancing. The other is itself two instruments, the second (*piffaro*) being mouth-blown by a separate player. This is the instrument associated with pastoral scenes of the Nativity. *Cornamusa*, a Sicilian name for the *zampogna*. *Piva*, a small bagpipe of northern Italy. *Sordellina*, an elaborate Neapolitan *zampogna* introduced about 1500.

FRANCE: *cornamuse*, a generic name for bagpipe. *Cabrette*, a name for the *cornamuse* in south and central France. It was favoured at court during the 17th and early 18th centuries. *Musette*, a bellows-blown bagpipe in use by the 17th century. *Biniou*, a peasant instrument of Brittany used in conjunction with a bass instrument, the *bombarde*.

FLANDERS: *muse-en-sac*, a bagpipe with one chanter and three drones, familiar from the 14th century to c. 1900.

ENGLAND: Northumbrian small pipes, dating from the late 17th century. An indoor instrument with an intimate sound, like a nasal oboe. It has a unique feature in that the chanter end is blocked to allow *staccato* playing.

SCOTLAND: three distinct types existed. The small-pipe was sometimes bellows-blown; the obsolete lowland pipe was played by a seated player; and the Highland pipe is the elaborately tasselled, tartan-bagged ceremonial instrument familiar today. The last mentioned has one chanter, two tenor drones and a bass drone.

IRELAND: union pipe, bellows-blown, played indoors for dancing or pure entertainment by a seated player. Its name may be derived from Gaelic *uilleann* ('elbow'), since the bellows are activated under the arm. It has been known since at least c. 1600.

WALES: *pibau cod*. No example is known. It was probably mouth-blown and it had a double chanter with two bells separated at the end. Introduced in the 12th century, it fell out of use by the 18th.

SPAIN: *gaita gallega*, a small bagpipe with single chanter and one long drone, found in north-west Spain. The name means 'Galician flute'. *Gaita* is a generic name for folk flute or oboe in the Iberian peninsula. A typical Spanish bagpipe would resemble the Scottish Highland pipe but with one drone.

Bass Horn

Louis Frichot, a French refugee to London from the Revolution of 1789, wisely decided that the serpent needed improvement. When he developed his instrument in the 1790s he called it 'English horn' to acknowledge his debt to his adopted country while causing confusion with the totally unrelated cor anglais. Now referred to, if at all, as 'bass horn', Frichot's instrument is a long copper tube doubled into the shape of a narrow 'V', and with a long crook leading to the mouthpiece. Its tone was best suited to outdoor and military bands, but by about 1835 it had been superseded by the *ophicleide* (see below).

THE ROMAN *CORNU* (LATIN FOR HORN). ITS REPORTED *SOTTO VOCE* TONE SUGGESTS IT WAS USED IN NUMBERS AS A PROCESSIONAL INSTRUMENT.

Black Pudding

With typical forthrightness, British North Country players of the serpent thus described their instruments. The leather covering of the serpent is likely to be dark brown than black in colour, but the overall impression of the instrument suggests the sinuous shape of the 'blood sausage' whose skin is black

Bladder-pipe

Using an animal bladder as an air reserve, the bladder-pipe is a primitive bagpipe, usually with just two pipes emerging, one to the mouth, the other carrying a raucous melody to the outside world.

Buccina

Dating from Roman times, this trumpet possessed a tuning slide and is thus an ancestor of the slide trumpet.

Chacocra

At least 2000 years old, the *chacocra* was a brass trumpet used in Jewish religious ceremonies.

Chalumeau

A French word meaning a bagpipe chanter (sounding pipe) with two reeds. The Nuremberg instrument-maker Denner applied the word to an instrument he was improving about 1700, thinking that it equated with shawm (English), *salmoe* (Italian) and *Schalmei* (German), an ancient instrument probably of Far Eastern origin. At the same time as carrying out these improvements, Denner was working on developing a hybrid instrument, a *chalumeau* plus-recorder. This became the clarinet. The *chalumeau* has a deeper, more throaty sound than the clarinet. The lower range of the clarinet is still called the '*chalumeau* register'.

Clarin

The inhabitants of Chile's Atacamá desert blow this long, straight trumpet like a flute: out at one side. Its primary use appears to be for signalling.

Cornet

A 19th-century brass instrument allied to the trumpet but now restricted mainly to brass and military bands. Not to be confused with cornett.

Cornett

A medieval instrument of wood or ivory with a pure, high tone suitable for church music or open-air serenades. In 1728 Roger North described its voice as eunuch-like. The cornett is usually gracefully curved, with an octagonal cross-section and finger holes; straight versions also existed. The Germans called it *Zink* (= the smallest tine of a stag's antlers), and to the French it was *cornet à bouquin* ('goat cornet').

Cornu

A long brass instrument shaped like a letter 'G', its crossbar extended to rest on the player's shoulder. The *cornu* originated in Tuscany (then Etruria), five centuries before Christ, and the Romans gave it a threatening dragon's mouth bell. The Roman poet Quintus Horatius Flaccus was impressed by its voice, which he described as "a menacing murmur".

℘ Crumhorn

A two-reed wooden instrument which enlivened the Middle Ages with its warm, mid-range voice, not heard since the 17th century except in modern 'authentic' bands. Its name, related to 'crumpled' or crooked, refers to its shape, which resembles a hockey stick with fingerholes.

℘ Jonkametótzi

A reed pipe from Peru, played cross-ways like a flute but lacking fingerholes. Instead, to control the note, a finger is inserted in the end.

℘ Karnyx

As the Iron-Age Celts closed for battle their enemies would have been cowed by the 2m (6.5 feet) long *karnyx*, a metal trumpet with a carved animal-horn bell that rose high above the player's head. If the battle were with the Danes, one might imagine the frightful din as *karnyx* player met *lur* player (see below), each inciting his fighting men with raucous bellows.

℘ Lichiguayo

An end-blown flute of Chile, 500 or more years old. A 'V'-shaped notch is cut at the upper end to facilitate sound production. Being of considerable length, its tone is low and seductive.

℘ Lituus

A Roman name for a pre-Roman bronze instrument shaped like a letter 'J'. Its straight conical pipe ended in a sharply-bent animal horn, and its use was probably mainly military.

℘ Lur

Thought of primarily as Danish, these large bronze trumpets were once widespread throughout Bronze Age northern Europe, where they had several uses: in battle, as a processional instrument and, in pairs, at religious festivals. In shape they resembled mammoth tusks. As noise makers they were effective; as musical instruments, mere curiosities.

♪ A MODERN *OCARINA* IN A DESIGN STANDARDIZED IN ITALY ABOUT 1860. THIS ELABORATE EXAMPLE IS MADE OF TERRACOTTA.

℘ Ocarina

Upper Egypt enjoyed the pure liquid tones of the *ocarina* 5000 years ago, when they were made of baked earth. Shaped like an elongated egg with a blowing-hole and fingerholes, they may still be bought today if one accepts plastic as a suitable substitute for mud. The name means 'little goose' in Italian. Modern examples are considerably slimmer than their predecessors. The voice is particularly attractive in that, unlike most wind instruments, the *ocarina* produces no overtones. This acoustic phenomenon is due to the globe-like shape of the instrument which allows the air within to vibrate as a whole when set in motion by blowing.

♪ MOST OF THE *OPHICLEIDE*'S HISTORY, OF ABOUT A CENTURY FROM 1821, UNFOLDED IN FRANCE, ITS COUNTRY OF ORIGIN.

℘ Ophicleide

This translates from the Greek as 'keyed serpent'. The instrument belies the antiquity its name suggests. Early in the 19th century efforts were made to improve the serpent (see bass horn, above); the best way was to replace it, which is what the Frenchman Halary did in 1821. As the bass voice of the cornet family the *ophicleide* was itself replaced by the bass tuba in orchestras. One Thomas Macbean Glen of Edinburgh invented a wooden version about 1850. He called it *serpentkleide*.

℘ Palawta

A six-hole flute of the Philippines, with slight variations in design between islands but wide differences in name. It is played cross-ways, as is the modern Western flute.

Panpipes
A PARALLEL EVOLUTION

It seems possible that panpipes evolved twice, independently. They were known in China (*p'ai-siao*) by 500 BC and in ancient Greece (*syrinx*) 1000 years earlier, where they were said to have been played to the water nymph Syrinx by Pan (hence their name). (Egyptian examples date from at least 330 BC.) From China panpipes spread throughout the Pacific and into South America, where they are known by various names:

CHILE (PRE-COLUMBIAN): *Laka*

PERU: *Anata; jonkari; urusa*

ARGENTINA, BOLIVIA, PARAGUAY, PERU: *Siku*, which, lacking a full chromatic range, require the melody to be divided between several players, giving a jerky stereo effect. Pipes may exceed 2m (6.5 feet) in length; they slant away from the player and rest on the ground.

From Greece, panpipes spread into the Balkans. Gheorghe Zamfir, the Romanian panpipes virtuoso, maintains that panpipes are the oldest of all musical instruments. He has composed a Concerto and a Rhapsody for them, and performances by him and his compatriots have widely popularized their virtuosic use in Romanian folk music. But they are to be heard at their most evocative in South American folk ensembles, where their haunting tones, together with the stomach-thumping rhythm of the *bomba* (large drum), seem to capture the atmosphere of high remote plains and snow-capped peaks.

Panpipes

Panpipes consist of a collection of pipes, graded in length and bound together side-by-side in a curved or straight pattern. The player blows across the top of each pipe in turn by moving his head or the pipes. The lower ends of the pipes are blocked. Panpipes are used for festive entertainments and dancing. Also see panel (left).

Pinkillo

The European recorder, being relatively easy to play, has given rise to local varieties. One, the *pinkillo* of Chile, is a small reed pipe with a mouthpiece; another, in Peru, is somewhat larger but bears the same name. Both produce clear tones, not unlike the familiar recorder family.

Putu or Pututu

Natural horns of great antiquity, played by the indigenous Indians of the Atacamá desert region of Chile. These horns, together with native trumpets and percussion, accompany ancient ritual songs sung in the pre-Columbian *kunza* language.

Quena

One of the most ancient of all flutes, the *quena* of Bolivia is an end-blown instrument made of bone, clay, reed or metal. In appearance and tone production it resembles the European recorder.

Recorder

We cannot know what the earliest recorders were called because nothing is known of the language spoken by the Middle Eastern peoples of the

A WELL-ORGANIZED (NOTE MICRO-PHONE!) STREET MUSICIAN WITH A SPECIES OF PANPIPES AND DRUM.

Upper Palaeolithic era, up to 27,000 years ago, who played the instrument, and even they may not have been the first. They constructed their end-blown instruments of reed, wood or bone, and a characteristic feature was, and remains today, the shape of the mouthpiece. This gave rise to the more recent Italian and German terms, *flauto a becco* and *Schnabelflöte* respectively, both meaning 'beak-flute'. Its pure tone attracted the French description *recordour*, bird-song imitation, from which our name derives. The recorder family is populous (see panel) as well as ancient in origin.

Shahnai

Common as an out-door instrument in North India (related instruments with similar names are found in Persia, Bangladesh and neighbouring areas), the *shahnai* is a two-reed oboe or shawm (the latter word derived from *shahnai*) with an extremely piercing sound. It is straight, with a small flared bell. Rather larger bells are found in the closely-related southern Indian *nagasvaram*.

℅ Shakuhachi

A Chinese bamboo flute, adopted by the Japanese, which may vary greatly in length. Its woody voice is capable of much variety and it can arouse emotional responses in the listener when played by an expert.

℅ Shofar

A ram's-horn trumpet bent into a 'J'-shape by the application of heat, sometimes equipped with a shaped end to act as a mouthpiece, and bearing sacred and/or secular inscriptions. Its main use is in Jewish religious ceremonies. The simple construction of the instrument limits it to very few notes, but these echo impressively within the synagogue to add solemnity to the occasion. It was probably *shofarot* (the correct plural) which sent Jericho's walls crashing down.

℅ Tiama

A long, low-pitched flute of Peru, made from bone, wood or reed.

A BASIC IMPALA-HORN TRUMPET FROM WHICH THE JEWISH LITURGICAL *SHOFAR* DEVELOPED (SEE TEXT).

℅ Trumpet

Widespread as an ethnic instrument. The term trumpet, used loosely, covers anything from the conch shell and *didgeridoo* to the modern valve instrument. Furthermore, large trumpets and small horns were virtually identical in the Middle Ages, and even into Baroque times. The principal difference between horn and trumpet during the developing years was that the trumpet was basically cylindrical until the abrupt flaring of the bell, while the horn was gently conical throughout its length until reaching the area of the, often larger, bell. This tended to give the horn a less piercing tone, though one may cite many exceptions in nomenclature, construction and sound production.

In pre-Roman days, simple straight tube-like trumpets were common throughout Africa and the East. They were used in hunting and battle but were unsuitable for indoor use. The situation changed by the Baroque period, when trumpeters and their drumming companions, from whom they were virtually inseparable, were honoured with special positions on platforms raised above the rest of the ensemble. ⑬

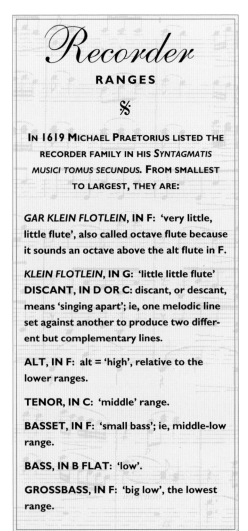

Recorder
RANGES
℅

IN 1619 MICHAEL PRAETORIUS LISTED THE RECORDER FAMILY IN HIS *SYNTAGMATIS MUSICI TOMUS SECUNDUS*. FROM SMALLEST TO LARGEST, THEY ARE:

GAR KLEIN FLOTLEIN, IN F: 'very little, little flute', also called octave flute because it sounds an octave above the alt flute in F.

KLEIN FLOTLEIN, IN G: 'little little flute'

DISCANT, IN D OR C: discant, or descant, means 'singing apart'; ie, one melodic line set against another to produce two different but complementary lines.

ALT, IN F: alt = 'high', relative to the lower ranges.

TENOR, IN C: 'middle' range.

BASSET, IN F: 'small bass'; ie, middle-low range.

BASS, IN B FLAT: 'low'.

GROSSBASS, IN F: 'big low', the lowest range.

INDIAN SILVER TRUMPET, OR *KARNA*, WHICH IS FOUND IN VARIABLE LENGTHS UP TO ABOUT 1.3 METRES (4 FEET).

PLUCKED INSTRUMENTS

STRINGS MAY be plucked by a variety of materials to produce a sharp but often rapidly decaying note. In the violin family the usual method is to pluck the string with the fingertip. In other instruments a plectrum may be used. This may be made of tortoiseshell, metal, wood or plastic. The plucking action in a harpsichord is achieved by a quill rising in response to the pressing of a key, plucking the string as it passes, then, in a configuration resembling a vertically elongated letter D, bypassing the string on its downward path before coming to rest.

Plucked stringed instruments are of extreme antiquity. Early in their history they divided into three families: lutes, harps and lyres. All three underwent diversification, but by far the most productive family was the lutes, which have

LEFT: THE CELEBRATED INDIAN SITARIST RAVI SHANKAR (SEE PAGE 24).
ABOVE: A JAPANESE BIWA, 1898, A TYPE OF PLUCKED LUTE; SEE PAGES 22–3.

Plucked Instruments

OCCASIONALLY HEARD IN CONCERT

❧

BALALAIKA The Russian composer Yuri Shushakov wrote a Balalaika Concerto (c. 1955) but representation of the instrument in concert and opera is most often made by imitation, as in Balakirev's Overture No. 1 on Russian Themes (1858, revised 1881).

BANJO Ernst Křenek's 'Little' Symphony, Op. 58 (1928) employs two banjos.

DOMBRA Nicolai Pavlovich Budashkin composed a concerto for Russian *dombra* in 1940.

GUSLI Rimsky-Korsakov required a plucked *gusli* to sound in his opera *Sadko* (1896), but the part is often taken instead by *pizzicato* strings.

GUITAR Famous guitar concertos have been written by Joaquín Rodrigo (in 1939), Mario Castelnuovo-Tedesco in the same year, André Previn (1971) and many others, and there is a Serenade (1955) by Malcolm Arnold. Boccherini transcribed six of his piano quintets for guitar, two violins, viola and cello in 1798–9 for the benefit of the guitar-playing Marquis de Benevente, and an early version (c. 1841) of Robert Schumann's Fourth Symphony includes one guitar in the slow movement.

JEW'S HARP Johann Heinrich Hörmann was apparently the first to welcome the Jew's harp into the recital room when he presented his Partita in C in about 1750. The instrument is accompanied by two recorders, four violins (two muted and two played *pizzicato*, to allow the strange visitor to be heard) and continuo. Around 1770 Johann Georg Albrechtsberger, later to be one of Beethoven's teachers, composed three concertos for what he termed *trombula* or *crembalum*. One of the works, for

trombula, harpsichord, violin, viola and cello, has been performed and recorded with a trumpet substituting for the *trombula*, a wildly anachronistic course since a trumpet of 1771 could not play the chromatic part Albrechtsberger wrote for the *trombula*. Furthermore, balance problems were acute. Light dawned when it was discovered that *trombula* and *crembalum* both referred to types of instrument in which several Jew's harps were attached to a frame.

KANTELE The Finnish composer Pehr Henrik Nordgren wrote a concerto, Op. 14, for clarinet, *kantele* and other Finnish folk instruments in 1970.

KITHARA Harry Partch composed his *Two Settings for Finnegan's Wake* (1944) for voice, flute and *kithara*.

MANDOLIN For an 'ethnic', and specifically Italian, instrument, the mandolin has been used widely by composers in many contexts and genres. Among the earliest, probably during the 1730s, were a solo concerto by Vivaldi (RV425) and another for two mandolins (RV532). After A. M. Bononcini used a mandolin in his opera *La conquista delle Spagne* (1707), the instrument travelled to England for Michael Arne's *Almena* (1764) and then to Germany three years later for J. G. Naumann's opera *L'Achille in Sciro*. Other operas have included it, among them Mozart's *Don Giovanni* (1787), Verdi's *Otello* (1887) and Pfitzner's *Palestrina* (1915). Mahler called for it in his Seventh and Eighth

Symphonies (1905; 1906). In the Seventh, together with guitar, it helps to create the nocturnal atmosphere of the fourth movement. In *Das Lied von der Erde* (1909), Mahler drew on its frail timbre for the unworldly landscape of the long final movement, 'Der Abschied'. Karl Amadeus Hartmann also required the mandolin in his Symphony No. 6 (1953).

OUD John Haywood recently collaborated with the Iraqi composer Salman Shukur on a concerto for *oud* and orchestra.

QANUN Muhammed Rifaat Garrana, the Egyptian composer, wrote a concerto for this instrument in 1967.

SANSA See Plucked Oddities, page 27. George Crumb, the American experimental composer, called for a *sansa* in his *Night of the Four Moons* (1966).

SITAR Ravi Shankar has written two concertos for *sitar*.

TOP: THE *BANJO*, POPULAR IN EARLY JAZZ, MUSIC HALLS AND, SOMETIMES, THE SYMPHONY.

BELOW: THE SUPREMELY PORTABLE AND EASILY PLAYED JEW'S HARP, THE ORIGIN OF WHOSE NAME REMAINS OBSCURE.

spread worldwide and given rise to innumerable varieties. Lyres have been dying out since about the 17th century, but harps are still current and very popular in both 'art' and folk music. The sound of a plucked string holds an abiding fascination for man. But, as will be seen, strings are not the only material which may be plucked in order to produce music.

✄ Baglama

A pear-shaped Turkish lute, found in various sizes in Turkey and played with a plectrum.

✄ Balalaika

A development of the lute (see *dombra*, below), the *balalaika* was known in Europe by the 17th century, when it appeared in several forms. It is now regarded as the national instrument of Russia, where the *balalaika* family underwent change during the modernization and regularization that took place in that country towards the end of the 19th century. The instrument's body shape was standardized to the familiar triangular form with three strings. The number

of sizes in which the family now comes is six: *piccolo, primo, secunda, viola, bass* and *contrabass*.

✄ Banjo

Sir Hans Sloane encountered a small lute in Jamaica and depicted it in a book written in 1688. He called the instrument *strum-strum*, a name lacking in imagination but indicative of what it sounded like. The *strum-strum* developed into the *banjo*, a name possibly derived from Spanish *bandore* via the French 18th-century *banza*. It became popular in the southern states of America (where it was called *banzer*), and later found a place in early jazz recordings because its piercing tone was easy to record and recognize. The body is round, with a skin resonator, and there are usually five strings. Hybrid *ukelele-banjos* of similar shape also exist; one example is mentioned below.

✄ Banjulele

A hydrid instrument of *banjo* and *ukelele*, invented by Albin and Kelvin Keech in 1925/6.

✄ Birimbao

A Jew's harp with a metal tongue in a pear-shaped metal frame, native to Cuba, Argentina, Brazil and other South American countries. In some of these countries the *birimbao* is known as the *trompa* or *trompe*. In Europe the Jew's harp is sometimes referred to as the 'Jew's trump' and this influence may be responsible for this alternative name. The name *birimbao* is doubtless of onomatopoeic origin.

✄ Charango

There were no stringed instruments in South America before the time of Christopher Columbus. The Spaniards brought their guitars with them and these were enthusiastically copied by the natives. The Bolivian *Quechua* Indians, for instance, created the *charango* at first from the shell of a small ground-burrowing armadillo. The drying shell of the animal was formed into a figure-of-eight shape, given a fingerboard and five double strings, and played like a guitar. So rapid was the spread of popularity of the *charango*, not only in Bolivia but in Peru, northern Argentina and other countries, that the armadillo was threatened with extinction until its hunting was banned by government. The subsequent change to wood as the principal material has brought dramatic variations in the size of the *charango*: some bodies are the size of a man's hand; others might be larger than that of a guitar. The name *charango* is said to be a corruption of the native term for armadillo: *quirkincho*.

𝄞 A RUSSIAN NAVY BAND PICTURED IN 1915. ALL SIZES OF *BALALAIKA* ARE SHOWN, THE LARGEST, SOMETIMES CALLED *DOMRA*, TAKING ITS NAME FROM AN EARLIER INSTRUMENT, THE *DOMBRA*, SEE PAGE 19.

℘ Crwth

A lyre-derived instrument originating in the western British Isles in the first century BC and surviving in Wales until the early 1800s. Its Celtic name was *cruit* or *crot*, the English name *crowd* or *crowth*. From c. 1300 the *crwth* was given a fingerboard and was bowed.

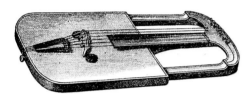

A WELSH *CRWTH*, WHICH SHOWS ELEMENTS OF BOTH THE VIOLIN AND THE LYRE.

℘ Dactylomonocordo

Meaning 'finger-one-string', this instrument was invented by a Neapolitan called Guida in about 1877, probably as an aid for music pupils.

℘ Dan Doc Huyen

This Vietnamese one-string *zither* is a rectangular box, slightly tapered and about one metre long. Near the left-hand end rises a stem with a gourd resonator from which runs a string which passes through the soundboard to a peg inside the box. The player carries a sliver of bamboo with which he plucks the string, meanwhile controlling the note with the outer edge of the other hand. The string tension is changed by pressing on the upright stem.

℘ Dan Tranh

A Vietnamese board *zither* with movable bridges and 16 steel strings, related to the Japanese *koto*.

℘ Dombra

This two-stringed lute may well have been the instrument from which the Russian *balalaika* derived. It is found in various forms in Kazakhstan, Kirghistan, Turkmenistan and Mongolia.

℘ Gottuvadyam

A south Indian modification of the *vina* (below), with a bowl and gourd upon which the instrument rests. The player plucks the strings and stops them with a wooden cylinder held in the left hand.

℘ Gurumi

A lute which was depicted on Ancient Egyptian tomb paintings and is still to be found, virtually unchanged, in Egypt today. It consists of a simple elongated body pierced by a fingerboard. The strings are not tuned by pegs but are bound by leather straps where the pegbox would have been.

℘ Gusli or Gussly

Confusion with the *gusle* or *gussli*, (names for the violin found in former Yugoslavia or primitive folk fiddle) is understandable, because the Slav word *gosl*, meaning strings, gave rise to both instruments. However, the presence of strings in both is their only point of similarity. The northwest Russian *gusli* is a large horizontal psaltery with up to 36 finger-plucked strings. It was familiar in Russia in the 18th century when Vasily Fyodorovich Trutovsky entertained the Russian aristocracy with his collection of folk tunes and original works on a *gusli*.

Jew's Harp

THE NAME

℘

Because of its supposedly humble origins, this instrument was said to be associated with beggars, who in turn were often regarded as Jewish immigrants reduced to being street musicians. There is no firm evidence for this, or for the name being a corruption of 'jaw's harp'; a possible derivation is from the Northern English name *jewjaw*, an onomatopoeia.

In Europe one encounters other names. *Munngiga* (Sweden) and *Maulgeige* (Germany) both mean 'mouth fiddle', the German *Maultrommel* means 'mouth drum', and early names suggest a connection with the trumpet: *trump*; *tromba*. This connection has been retained in many non-European names for the instrument.

℘ Jew's Harp

As a small pocket instrument, cheap to buy and rewarding to play, the Jew's harp has been popular for centuries and over a wide area. The familiar instrument comprises a metal flagon- or pear-shaped body and a central tongue plucked with the finger. When put to the mouth the instrument's weak tone is amplified by the mouth cavity and the note is modified as the lips move. Varieties are widespread in the Pacific region, India, Asia and Europe, some dating from 2000 years ago, or even more in Egypt. They might be made of metal, wood (bamboo and palm are found), bone or ivory. The European metal model has been exported to many peoples, including the North American Indians, who made copies locally.

♆ Kerar

An Ethiopian bowl lyre, in which a circular bowl made from tortoise shell or some cooking utensil supports the two arms which in turn support the yoke to which the strings are attached. Often heavily decorated, the *kerar* is used by tribal doctors to drive out the evil spirits of a sick person using music, incantations and the supposed magical powers of the decorations which may include mirrors and charms.

♆ Kinnor

Pictorial representations of King David playing a 'harp' actually show a *kinnor*, a type of lyre.

♆ Kithara

An ancient Greek lyre made of a wooden resonator and, usually, seven strings which were tuned by adjusting their tension rather than their length. From its Middle Eastern origins, the *kithara* became immensely popular in Greece, where both Apollo and Orpheus are said to have

♆ Kantele

A Finnish psaltery reputed to be 2000 years old. In its early form the *kantele* consisted of a horizontal board up to 80cm (31 inches) long, a maximum of 40cm (16 inches) wide tapering to about 10cm (4 inches), and with up to ten metal or gut strings running along its length. Their tuning pegs lie below the wider end, which is usually angled to accommodate the different lengths of the strings. Hitherto characterized by a weak voice and limited range, the instrument has latterly undergone conversion into a concert instrument thanks to a number of improvements during the 20th century, including an increase in the number of strings. The Finnish composer Martti Pokela has helped preserve the *kantele* tradition at the Sibelius Academy and has composed several works for the instrument.

♪ ABOVE: GREEK TERRACOTTA STATUETTES FROM THE 3RD CENTURY AD. THE MAIDEN ON THE LEFT PLAYS A *KITHARA* (LYRE) TO THE ACCOMPANIMENT OF A SLENDER LUTE.

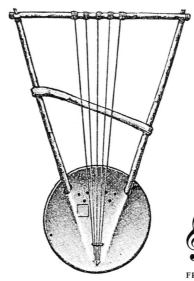

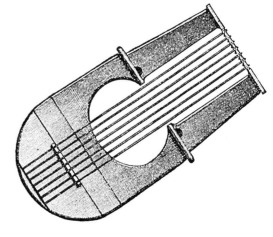

♪ A PRIMITIVE LYRE (LEFT) FROM ETHIOPIA COMPARED TO A MORE DEVELOPED TYPE FROM GREECE. IT IS EASY TO IMAGINE HOW THE FORMER DERIVED FROM THE SKULL AND HORNS OF AN ANIMAL.

played it, and where it served as accompaniment to epic songs of mythical adventures, and eventually this popularity travelled with it to Rome. Mark Anthony so admired the playing of Anaxemor that he put a military guard at his disposal and awarded him the rights to levy tribute on four Roman cities. Two *kithara* players visiting Rome so impressed the normally parsimonious Emperor Vespasian that he paid them 200 000 *sesterces*, and Nero awarded the *kithara* player Menecrates with a palace and a fortune. Although itself a lyre, the *kithara* developed a separate existence, so that writers refer to it as 'supplanting the lyre' in popularity. The word *kithara* is influential. It is almost certainly the root of both *guitar* and *zither*, and may have influenced *sitar* (see page 25).

✺ Konting

A five-stringed lute of the *Mandinka* people of the Gambia. It is a diminutive instrument, oval-bodied and with an animal-skin membrane.

✺ Kora

An instrument of West African origin, most commonly found in the Gambia. Its hybrid design is reflected in the description 'harp lute'. A large leather-covered gourd resonator is pierced by a long neck which supports 21 strings. These, divided 10-11, run down in two courses to a flat horizontal bridge protruding from the gourd towards the player, always male, who plucks the strings with his fingers. Two wooden dowel handles emerge from the gourd upwards at an angle and close to the strings. In performance the *kora* has a wide range of sounds. Not only are melody and accompaniment combinations possible but the player will sometimes flick his fingers against the handles to produce a percussive rhythm. This is further enhanced when a colleague strikes the rear of the gourd with a stick. Particularly charming aspects of the *kora* are the attachment of jingles to the bridge, and a hole in the gourd to accept monetary contributions.

THIS **1898** REPRESENTATION OF A *KOTO* PLAYER CONVEYS THE ATMOSPHERE OF A MORE LEISURELY AGE IN JAPANESE COURTS. TO PLAY *KOTO* WITH DELICACY WAS THE AIM OF MANY A YOUNG WOMAN OF GOOD BIRTH.

THE Kantele Family

✺

DESPITE BEING RESTRICTED TO THE NORTH-EAST CORNER OF EUROPE AND SURROUNDING COUNTRIES, THE FINNISH *KANTELE* HAS DEVELOPED IN SEVERAL DIRECTIONS:

✺

ESTONIA
KANNEL: A hollow tree trunk surmounted by a flat soundboard, with half-a-dozen plucked strings.

LATVIA
KOKLE: Similar originally to the Estonian *kannel*, but now made in four sizes, with metal strings up to 26 in number replacing the earlier gut strings.

LITHUANIA
KANKLES: Similar to, but generally smaller than, the original Finnish *kantele*, the *kankles* possesses up to ten strings.

NORTH-WEST RUSSIA
GUSLI: Early *guslis* in north west Russia had up to 14 strings; later versions are more developed. See *gusli*.

✺ Koto

Originally from China, where a similar instrument called *cheng* still exists, the *koto* is now regarded as specifically Japanese. It was introduced to Japan in the 8th century AD and has remained basically unchanged ever since. It is a 2m (6.5 feet) long wooden *zither*, placed horizontally in front of the player who plays the 13 silk strings (though nylon is increasingly used) with fingertips or plectra. Each string has a dedicated bridge which is movable for tuning. Related varieties of the *koto* are still found in China, and in Korea.

Lute, Lyre and Harp
ESSENTIAL DIFFERENCES

LUTE In its basic form the lute consists of a sound table, usually of wood. This comprises the fingerboard (with or without frets) and the upper face of the resonating body. Strings run parallel to the sound table; they are attached by tuning pegs at the upper end, run across a bridge on the resonating body and are then attached at the lower end. The resonating body may be of virtually any shape and is, of course, hollow, sometimes with holes or slots in the upper face. Lutes may be plucked (like the *banjo*) or bowed (like the violin).

LYRE Instead of running parallel with a fingerboard, the lyre's strings are attached to a yoke which is held away from the sound table by two struts, making, with the table, four sides of a square, or, in some models, an 'H' shape. Thus, the strings run freely through the air between the yoke and the sound table. This table, as in the lute, is a resonating box which may be of any shape and may be pierced by a soundhole. Bowed lyres are rare. See also *kithara*.

HARP Non-Western and ancient harps fall into three categories:

ARCH HARP (or bow harp): the earliest and most primitive type, is a gracefully curved wooden bow to which strings are attached twice at different points along its length. A resonator is usually attached to, or is part of, the bow.

ANGLE HARP: possibly a slightly later design than the arch harp but certainly of pre-Christian date, the angle harp is an 'L'-shaped structure, across the angle of which runs a number of strings. A resonator may form either arm of the 'L'-shaped body.

FRAME HARP: first depicted in the 8th century AD, the frame harp is a structure in the shape of a 'V' with a closed top and is therefore more robust in construction than the other types. Strings run from one side of the 'V' (which also houses the resonator) to the enclosing bar at the top. It is from this design that the modern harp developed. Harps are always plucked; the structure of all three types would make bowing impracticable.

AN ANCIENT EGYPTIAN BOW HARP COMPLETE WITH BOWL RESONATOR WHICH SUPPORTS THE CARVED HEAD OF A NOBLE FIGURE.

✄ Lute

From its prehistoric origins somewhere in the Middle East, the plucked lute has undergone vast diversification, too vast in fact for more than a sample to be discussed here. Its wide distribution, too, defeats detailed examination in a general book, but if we endeavour to follow its names along geographical lines it may help to illustrate its spread.

A representation on a Mesopotamian seal of about 2000 BC may show a long-necked lute; more decisive of its early existence are Egyptian paintings of about a thousand years later, by when the lute was well established throughout the Middle East. The Egyptian pictograph, a circle from which rose a vertical line cut by two short horizontal lines, represents the non-vowel sound *n-f-r* and is a certain illustration of a stringed instrument. Later Egyptian words included *a'guz* (cf. Yugoslav *gusle*), while the Arabian word *al'ud* ('flexible stick') gave rise to *outi* and *laghoute* (Greece), *liuto* and *lutina* (Italy), *laud* (Spain), *luth* (France); *Laute* (Germany) and *lute* (England). Arab-Moroccan *gunibri* and Sudanese *gunbri* are clearly related, and the Arab *kobus* and *qabus* probably gave rise to *gambus* and *kabosa*, found in both North Africa and Asia, the *kobza* of Romania and the *qupuz* of eastern Europe. The North African *quitara* led to the

Italian *chitarra* and *chitarrone* and thence to *cistre* (France), *Cithrinchen* and *Erzcistre* (Germany), *cittern* (Europe), *cithare, citole* and *cither* (England) and guitar. Local names also arose: *tanpur, tanbur* and *dambura* are found in Afghanistan, Turkey, Pakistan, and may be the root of Indian *tambura* and Georgian *panturi,* while Italian *bandola, mandola, mandolin, mandora,* etc probably became

pandora and *pandurina* in the rest of Europe, the *pandurion* in Greece, and *Mandürchen* in Germany. In India the *mayuri* and *tayus* both mean 'peacock' (Sanskrit and Hindustani respectively) which suggests the shape of the instrument. Further east, China developed its own words for different lute-type instruments: *pi'pa, san hsien, shuang ch'in, su hu,* etc; and in Japan are found *chicuzen,*

The Lute
HOW MANY STRINGS?

𝄇

THE EARLIEST KNOWN REFERENCE TO THE LUTE IS DATED 3000 BC. ORIGINALLY THE NAME WAS *TAR* (AN ARMENIAN LUTE IS CALLED BY THAT NAME TO THIS DAY). PERSIA PROVIDED THE FOLLOWING DEFINITIONS WHICH, SADLY (SEE *SITAR*), HAVE BEEN MISUNDERSTOOD IN SOME AREAS:

𝄇

TAR	= 'stringed'
DUTAR	= 'two-stringed'
SITAR	= 'three-stringed'
CARTAR	= 'four-stringed'
PANCTAR	= 'five-stringed'

gekkin, genkwan, ku, satsuma and *shamisen.*

The body of the European lute resembles a pear cut in half, its rounded back made up of ribs of wood. The soundboard bears a 'rose', a soundhole under the courses of paired strings. The fretted fingerboard terminates in a pegboard angled downwards almost at right-angles. Largely superseded in the 19th century by the guitar, the lute has undergone a strong revival in the 20th century in the hands of such artists as Julian Bream and the revived interest in early music in general.

𝄞 A LATE EXAMPLE OF A LYRE IN A ROMANTIC EARLY 19TH CENTURY DOMESTIC SETTING. BY THEN, THE LYRE WAS AN ANACHRONISTIC CURIOSITY.

� Musical Bow

A simple instrument of Papua New Guinea, some 30cm (12 inches) long, comprising a vegetable fibre attached either at both ends of a bow or at one end and hooked round a notch to provide two playing strings. The instrument's weak tone reduces its suitability for musical uses other than private amusement.

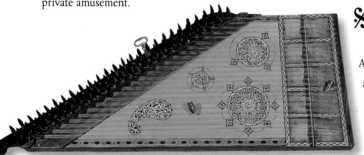

A TYPE OF PSALTERY FROM DAMASCUS, THE *QANUN* BEARS ONE OF MANY DIFFERENT NAMES FOR SIMILAR INSTRUMENTS IN OTHER AREAS.

✻ Nanga

A *trough zither* of Tanzania. *Trough zithers* are made of a piece of wood hollowed out longitudinally with strings attached at each end, wound round slits in the wood. The hollow trough acts as a resonator when the strings are plucked.

✻ Oud

An Arabic lute of five strings, without frets. The name may be the (French-influenced) version of Arabic *al'ud* ('flexible stick'), from which 'lute' was derived.

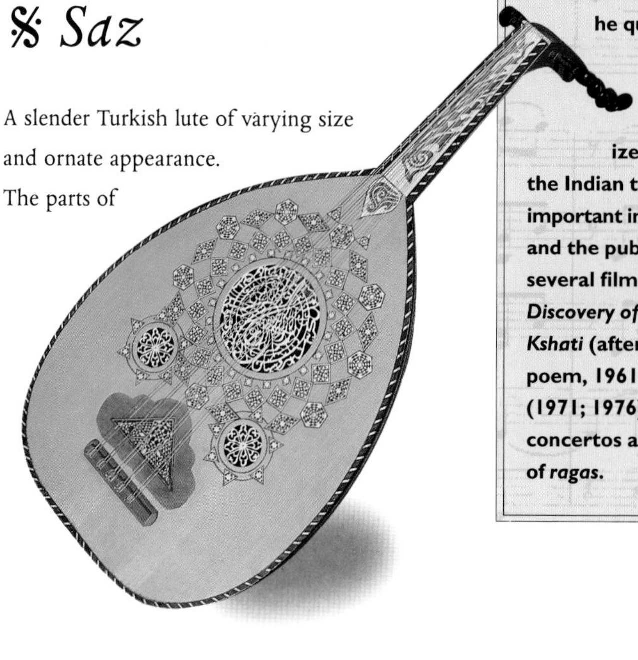

AN *OUD*. THIS EXAMPLE IS A 'SHORT LUTE', IN CONTRAST TO THE 'LONG LUTE', THE TURKISH *COLASCIONE*, PICTURED ON PAGE 22.

✻ Psaltery

A dulcimer-type instrument of considerable antiquity, being a flat box with plucked strings. The word 'psaltery' may be from the Greek *psaltein* (to pluck), or from the instrument's role in accompanying the psalms.

✻ Qanun

An Arab instrument found in Egypt and many points east, the *qanun* is a psaltery. The strings, which may number up to 100, are played with plectra. Said to have been invented during the tenth century, it spread across the Mediterranean and has enjoyed sporadic popularity in Middle Eastern countries ever since. For two centuries, starting in the 13th century, the *qanum* was played with its back against the player's chest instead of, as before and since, being placed across the player's knees.

✻ Robab

A six-stringed long lute of Afghanistan.

✻ Saz

A slender Turkish lute of varying size and ornate appearance.
The parts of

Ravi Shankar

✻

Western awareness of Indian music was awoken for the first time in the 1950s due to the tireless championship of Ravi Shankar. It continues largely by later artists following his example. Shankar was born in Uttar Pradesh in 1920 and first came to Europe and the United States on tour in 1956–7. He gave three sell-out performances at the Edinburgh Festival in 1963. Western musicians quickly discovered the value of Indian music through Shankar's performances, Yehudi Menuhin becoming involved enough to travel to India and to record duets with Shankar in classic 'East-meets-West' programmes. In the popular scene, too, there were experiments with Eastern philosophies and Indian music, most notably by The Beatles, under the influence of George Harrison, in 'Within You Without You' from their album *Sergeant Pepper's Lonely Hearts Club Band*. Harrison appeared with Shankar at the Woodstock Festival in August 1969.

Shankar began as a musician and dancer under the guidance of his elder brother Uday. Later, a more formal musical education was secured with Ustad Allauddin Khan and Ali Akbar Khan, after which he quickly rose to become the foremost *sitar* virtuoso. Critics have found his later performances to be too stylized and virtuosic to be true to the Indian tradition, but he remains an important influence on Western musicians and the public. He has also composed several film scores, ballet music including *Discovery of India* (1944) and *Samanya Kshati* (after Rabindranath Tagore's poem, 1961) and two concertos for sitar (1971; 1976). He has recorded these concertos and made many recordings of *ragas*.

the *saz* are connected with Islamic religious symbolism: the body of the instrument represents Ali, the fourth caliph of Islam, the neck is his sword, and when twelve strings are present they are the twelve prayer leaders of Islam. *Saz* is also the generic Turkish word for musical instrument, but in Russia and the former Yugoslavia the word specifies the long-necked lute.

❧ *Sitar*

Together with the double drum, the *tabla*, the *sitar* is regarded in the West as the quintessence of Indian music. It retains elements of both lute and *zither* design but has reached a stage of high sophistication. A thick fingerboard terminates at the lower end in a bulbous body. At the upper end a resonator gourd of almost equal size balances the instrument while lending it an ungainly appearance when played. Of the seven strings, two are drones; there are a further 12 or more sympathetic strings running inside the neck, and there are metal frets. The origin of the *sitar* is obscure, and further obscured by the name, which means 'three-stringed'. If the instrument derives from the Persian *setar* (also meaning 'three-stringed') it has evolved quite dramatically, for the *setar* was, confusingly, a four-stringed lute of slender construction with a small wooden resonating body and a thin neck.

❧ *Tambura*

An Indian lute with four unstopped metal strings. The open strings are plucked to provide a drone accompaniment.

❧ *Vambi*

A primitive arch harp consisting of a resonator of wood and animal skin from which run four strings to tuning pegs on a gently-curving stem. This is one of hundreds of varieties of arch harp found around the world; its use is limited to the *Bateke* tribe of Central Africa.

❧ *Vanniyayar*

(Also *muhonyu, quongon,* etc) A Siberian Jew's harp which, unlike others of this description, does not rely upon the mouth cavity to provide resonance. Instead, the bulb-shaped end, which terminates and joins two parallel metal bars, is held while a metal tongue lying between them is activated by the finger. The sound produced is a loose, high-pitched rattle rich in overtones. Players, usually female, are adept at producing a range of tones.

❧ *Vaz*

An Afghan arch harp comprising a bow set like a letter 'U' in a firm, flat base. The four strings are plucked with the fingertips.

❧ *Vicitra Vina*

A large Hindustani *zither* of substantial construction. One end of the table bears a bowl, the other

a heavily-made pegbox, and the whole is supported on two huge gourd resonators. The plucked strings are stopped with an egg-shaped glass globe in the left hand.

❧ *Vina*

A long-necked lute of southern India with a large body and a gourd resonator of equal size attached behind the pegboard. There are seven strings, three of which are drones.

❧ *Zither*

The term *zither* defines a stringed instrument distinct from lute, lyre and harp in that any resonating device may be detached from the *zither* without making it unplayable. A *zither* in its basic form, therefore, consists of a stick with strings running parallel with it, and frets to raise

the strings away from the stick and to provide 'stopping' points for the fingers of the player. This type is called a *stick zither*. The strings may be plucked or struck; in some rare examples they are bowed. Frets in the form of raised blocks of wood may number as few as three or more than a dozen.

The south Indian *vina* is classed as a lute because the lower resonator has over the centuries become an integral part of the isntrument and cannot be removed. In northern India an equivalent instruments, the *bin* (the two words are clearly related) is a *zither* because the gourd resonators, usually two but sometimes three in number, may be detached. This removal will, of course, affect the strength and quality of the instrument's tone but the *bin* will remain playable.

In the *tube zither*, fibres from the wooden tubular body are detached and raised on shallow bridges to form strings. These are common in Madagascar but probably originated in South-East Asia. When several *tube zithers* are bound side-by-side a *raft zither* is created, a form popular in several areas of Africa. (For the *trough zither*, see *nanga*, above.) A *board zither* comprises a rectangular board, which may include a box or gourd resonator, carrying a number of strings end-to-end. Bridges raise the strings off the face of the board. This type of design shades off into the psaltery family, where the box may vary from the rectangular; see *qanum*, page 24.

More advanced are the so-called *long zithers*, such as the *koto* (above), the Burmese *mi gyuan* (ingeniously constructed to resemble a crocodile with an arched back), and the European *zithers* which have become popular in Austrian, French, German and the folk cultures of other nations. Strictly speaking, harpsichord, spinet and virginals are sophisticated examples of *zither* in which the strings are plucked mechanically rather than by the fingers. Struck *zithers*, such as the dulcimer, are dealt with under Banged Instruments. The Aeolian harp is also a type of *zither* (see page 42).

METHODS OF
Plucking

There are two methods of plucking a stringed instrument: by the fingers or with a plectrum (plural: plectra) attached to or held by the fingers.

FINGER Some instruments, such as the harp, are plucked by the fingertips since they need a delicate, sensitive touch, although on occasion these call for a sharper, more incisive sound. For some compositions the harp strings are 'stroked' by the flesh of the fingertips to make a ghostly *glissando* effect.

FINGERNAILS In Eastern countries, and indeed elsewhere, musicians will sometimes let their fingernails grow extremely long and tough, the better to sound plucked instruments. In certain circumstances, on instruments with wound wire strings, composers will ask for a grating *glissando*, achieved when the string is scratched longitudinally by the fingernails.

PLECTRUM The Romans called this playing technique *plectrum*, which was also one of their words for lyre; the method of playing thus transferred to the instrument itself. Plectra may be made from virtually any hard but slightly yielding material. Wood, bone, reed, ivory and tortoiseshell were common, and the quill of a feather continued to be used for many years as the plucking component of the harpsichord. Modern harpsichord plectra of plastic are still called quills. In the Middle Ages plectra were called *penna*, a word which relates to 'pen', also made from quills. Large birds also provided plectra from their beaks and talons.

A plectrum in the shape of a flat egg with a sharply pointed end is used by banjo and ukulele players, and other shapes, elongated but with an easily-held widening are found. Mandolin players used to use pointed plectra of overall thin design which protruded beyond the backs of the fingers, but most are held between thumb and forefinger. Japanese *shamisen* players use plectra some 25cm (10 inches) long, widened at the playing end and narrowing to form a handle held in the palm of the hand. (The illustration of a 19th-century *shamisen* player below shows the abnormally large plectrum.)

Other types fit over the finger and thumb, effectively lengthening and strengthening both for prolonged playing of wire-strung instruments. Players of psalteries and horizontal *zithers* will use thimble-type or ring plectra which fit over the end of the finger and thumb or slide to between the first and second joint, with extensions beyond the ends of the digits.

🎼 PLUCKED ODDITIES

🎼 Ektara

Used as an accompaniment to singing, the *ektara* of Bangladesh consists of a gourd or small drum to which is fastened the two split sides of a bamboo stem. A string runs from the centre of the drum to the dividing node of the bamboo and is plucked with the fingers. A lower note may be obtained when the end of the bamboo is pressed to relax the string. The *ektara* also rejoices in alternative names: *gopijantra* and *gupijantra*. A similar Indian instrument is called *gopiyantra*.

🎼 Ground Harp

In central Africa the natives will tie a string to a flexible stem either growing or planted in the ground. The other end is led down to a soundboard fixed over a small pit with a weight or a system of pegs. The string, under tension from the stem, is then plucked with the fingers and resonates dully in the pit. Some tribes prefer to hit the string with sticks and/or play upon the soundboard with beaters. There is only slight musical value in the result; mainly the instrument gives delight to children. In Bangladesh a portable version is called *ananda lahari*.

🎼 Kalumbu Bow

A *zither* of central Africa which goes under many different names, indicating its extreme antiquity. It originated as a hunter's bow to which was affixed a resonator (gourd or cooking pot) and a single string to be plucked by a finger. Really sophisticated models attached a second string, but some Africans drew music from smaller models of it by attaching a cord and whirling it round their heads. This had the effect of raising the player's reputation because he was then capable of creating mysterious sounds out of the air. Compare *bull-roarer*, page 42.

🎼 Khamak

A small wooden cylinder, about 17cm (6.7 inches) in diameter, is held under the left arm of a Bangladeshi musician, who holds a string in his left hand. This string passes through the open end of the cylinder and is flexed with the fingers. The right hand strums the string with a plectrum. This variety of string drum is also called *gubgubi*. A similar instrument in India is also called *khamak*.

🎼 Sansa

Also called *kaffir piano, likembe, mbira, zeze, thumb piano*, etc, the *sansa* is named after the Congolese tribe among whom it was first discovered by Western explorers. The instrument probably arose several centuries before the 16th, the date of the earliest extant examples. The *sansa* resembles a flat wooden box (which might be of almost any size) from one side of which emerge a series of metal plates at a shallow angle. These plates are sprung down and released by the fingers and thumbs of the player to produce a liquid, twanging sound. 𝄢

🎼 IN ANCIENT GREECE, POETRY AND SONG WERE USUALLY INSEPARABLE. HERE, SAPPHO AND ALCAEUS PERFORM TO THEIR OWN ACCOMPANIMENT OF LYRES.

BANGED INSTRUMENTS

THIS IS THE SIMPLEST and most primitive way to sound an instrument. Infants do not need to be taught how to do it. The instrument is, quite simply, hit by another object. Drums and gongs of almost every type may be attacked by any means, ranging from the lightest tap of a fingernail to a blow with a heavy object that would kill a man.

A drum, singular, comprises two components, a body and a head. The body may be of virtually any hollow shape which contains air, and the head may be made from a large variety of materials. When the head is hit, it vibrates: this in turn induces vibration in the air which is amplified by the body. Some drums have two 'heads', one at each end of the body; others have one head, the other end being either open or enclosed by an extension of the body. A few drums do not have a hollow body: they resound when their solid material is struck.

In instruments which are sounded by hitting (and drums are by no means the only ones), the basic idea is the same: to strike the instrument – with stick, hand, fist, whip, or whatever 'beater' is chosen – with the intention of making it resound. The sounds produced are of unimaginable variety; see Gong, page 33.

The range and variety of 'banged' instruments is so vast that only a selection may be mentioned here. Africa alone would yield enough types to fill this entire book. Indeed, Africa may be called the 'Drum Continent', because nowhere else in the world has a greater range or number of drums. Africa was the continent which saw the emergence of man and probably the beginning of music itself. It is almost certain that the first musical instrument was a drum, and from that beginning arose a whole galaxy of struck instruments. Together with drums, wind and stringed instruments are common in Africa, and all have been used for similar purposes, though variations exist in different cultural areas. Drums predominate in the following activities:

✀ Dance

Tribal rites, births, marriages, and other events of a joyful nature are almost unthinkable without the sound of instruments, and since the native African appreciates rhythm above all other musical utterances, drums are their favourite instruments.

✀ Speech

Human speech, itself basically rhythmic among most of the 1000 or so languages found in Africa, is imitated in music. The best examples are the various types of so-called 'message drums' or 'talking drums' that carry brief messages through forests and for long distances across the plains.

YORUBA COURT DRUMMERS OF SOUTH-WEST NIGERIA, IN TRADITIONAL FORMAL DRESS.

War

Inter-tribal conflicts were, and still are, accompanied by preliminary bouts of drumming to stir up loyal emotions. Drum rhythms become insistent during the battles themselves to instil excitement and passion in the warriors and terror in their enemies.

Ceremony

Whether this is the installation of a new chief, the arrival of important visitors, or the funeral rites of an elder, drums will accompany it. They may be joined by joyful or doleful horn and trumpet sounds and the chanting or wailing of the tribe.

Talking drums, African style

African languages operate on two levels: rhythmic speech and tonal inflexion. Combined, these may be interpreted by differently-pitched drums or single log drums capable of producing more than one pitch, any ambiguities becoming clear by intelligent appreciation of the context. Message drums are used for short messages. They may warn of danger, though the nature of the danger may not be obvious. They may call the tribe home for some important meeting, or they may signal success in a hunt. Not many syllables are needed, then, for simple messages such as 'Look out!', 'Come home', or 'I have killed'. The continuous rattle of 'talking' drums which so unnerves explorers are not extended messages but the same message repeated over and over.

ZOLTAN KODALY, WHOSE *HARY JANOS* SUITE MAKES PROMINENT USE OF *CIMBALOM*, WITH HIS SECOND WIFE SAVOLTA AND A PUPIL IN 1960.

Banged Instruments
OCCASIONALLY HEARD IN CONCERT

ANVIL The sharp incisive sound of hammer on anvil is required, of course, in Verdi's 'Anvil' Chorus from *Il Trovatore* (1853), in Wagner's *Siegfried* (1876) and in Jón Leif's 'Saga' Symphony (1943); other composers have called for it, none more so than Wagner, who required 18 in *Das Rheingold* (1869).

BELLS These have featured in countless works since the 18th century, but Tchaikovsky outdid every other composer by requesting that "all the bells of Moscow" be rung during his *1812* Overture (1880). More conventionally, composers have called for tubular bells to provide such effects; their low, baleful tolling at the end of Shostakovich's Symphony No. 11 (1957) provides a good example of their effectiveness.

BONGOS The French-born American Edgard Varèse was among many composers who have required the sound of bongos: his *Ionisation* (1931) includes them in the complement of 13 percussion instruments.

BRAKE DRUM John Cage and others have sought the ringing tones of a struck suspended car brake drum in their works. His

First Construction (in Metal) (1939) includes them along with cowbells, sleighbells, gongs and anvils.

CIMBALOM The most famous example of the use of a *cimbalom* in the orchestra is in Kodály's *Hary Janos* Suite (1927).

GONG Gongs have been used in the orchestra since Gossec's *Funeral Music* (1791). The orchestral *tam-tam*, too, features regularly in scores. The gong has, however, occasionally been given an unusual role, for example when it is played by a violin bow – in Penderecki's *Dimensions der Zeit und der Stille* ('Dimensions of Time and Silence', 1960) – or made to produce a *glissando* by being lowered into a tub of water (in works by Lou Harrison and John Cage).

SHIELD In his 'Saga' Symphony of 1943, the Icelandic composer Jón Leifs included several ancient instruments including struck shields.

TABOR A long, narrow drum of high pitch, used in Bizet's *L'Arlesienne* Suite (1873) and Copland's *El Salon Mexico* (1933) and *Appalachian Spring* (1945)

℘ *Adapu*

A rectangular frame drum from Sumeria, some 7000 years old.

℘ *Ala Bohemica*

A 14th-century psaltery of Bohemia: the name means 'Bohemian wing'. The flat wing-shaped table has two soundholes. At one end of the table stands a half-moon wooden block through which strings pass, to be secured at the far end. The strings are played with small beaters.

℘ *Alal*

A Sumerian frame drum, larger than the *adapu*.

℘ *Anvil*

The blacksmith's anvil produces a loud metallic clang when struck and has done so ever since metal was first worked in a forge. Occasionally, this sound is requested by composers to produce a particularly harsh percussive effect.

℘ *Atumpan*

Large conical drums of Ghana, sometimes carried on the shoulder of one man while another strikes it with sticks; at other times the player hangs it round his neck on a cord and plays it himself. On the Ivory Coast the instruments are called *atungblan*: they are played in pairs and used for signalling and as talking drums.

℘ *Balag*

A perhaps slightly inaccurate rendering of the Sumerian generic word for 'drum'.

℘ *Baz*

A name still used for the Arab small kettledrum and probably identical with the word known by the Ancient Egyptians of the Middle Kingdom, c. 2100 to 1600 BC.

℘ *Bell*

A familiar instrument, in which a metal bowl is either inverted and suspended to swing so that the clapper inside strikes the inner surface, or is held still and struck upon the outside by strikers. In Ghana, conical bells are held aloft and struck with sticks; another design has a boat-shaped bell held in the hand and struck with an iron rod. The closing or opening of the hand controls the amount and quality of tone required.

♪ MODERN AFRICAN DRUMMERS. THE LONG, SINGLE-HEADED BARREL DRUMS PRODUCE A VARIETY OF TONES DEPENDING UPON THE STRENGTH OF THE FINGER STRIKES AND THEIR POSITIONS ON THE SKINS.

℘ *Bendir*

A round frame drum, about 50cm (20 inches) in diameter, of western North Africa, in which one or two snares (wires) pass under the single head. These give the tone added bite and carrying power.

℘ *Bombo*

A large barrel drum, about 60cm (24 inches) in diameter, with two goatskin heads, found in military and folk bands of Chile, Argentina and other South American countries. The player may strike the frame as well as the head.

℘ *Bongo*

Vellum-headed drums familiar in Latin American dance music. Descended from pre-Columbian models, these small, basin-shaped drums are often joined in pairs. They are held on the knees and played with the fingers. Their pitch is high and penetrating.

℘ *Boobams*

Recent North American development of the *bongo*: a series of chromatically-tuned drums with resonators (of bamboo, hence the name) of varying length.

℘ *Brake Drum*

Literally a car part, suspended and hit to produce a resonant, bell-like tone.

℘ *Cai Bong*

An hourglass drum of Vietnam but with only one head, played with the hands.

✵ Caja

A South American frame drum with two heads and snares, frequently found in Argentina, Bolivia, Chile, Colombia and Paraguay. It may reach 50cm (20 inches) in diameter. The body is of wood, sometimes of tin, and the skins are fastened by crossed cords. The word *caja* is also known in Cuba where it signifies the lead instrument of a percussion group.

✵ Changgo

A wooden hourglass drum with heads of about 40cm (16 inches) in diameter and played horizontally. The head on the left is of cowhide and played by hand, that on the right is of horsehide and played with a bamboo striker.

✵ Chang-ku

A Chinese drum in which the two heads extend beyond the diameter of the body and cords run between the heads. These cords, in 'W' pattern, are tightened and relaxed by metal rings to tune the drum.

✵ Ch'uk

A wooden box of approximately rectangular shape with a hole in the top lid. Korean musicians thrust a stick through the hole and strike the floor of the box in a rhythmic pattern.

TOP: EGYPTIAN CLAPPERS OF THE 18TH DYNASTY (1600-1400 BC). RIGHT: TIBETAN MONKS CHANTING TO THE RHYTHM OF THE *ROL-MO*, METAL CYMBALS WHOSE LARGE CENTRAL BOSSES CONTRIBUTE TO THEIR LOUD TONE.

✵ Cimbalom

A Hungarian struck dulcimer, a horizontal rectangular or trapeziform box of strings, originally an early folk instrument but since improved (during the 1860s) to bring it up to recital standard, with dampers and a wide chromatic range.

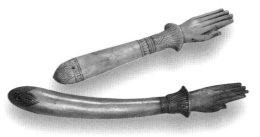

✵ Clappers

The Egyptians of c. 1460 BC fashioned wood or ivory into representations of human forearms and hands, then clapped them together during musical entertainments. Similar effects are obtained in the Balkans, the Middle East and Asia, where the objects might vary from spoons to brooms, one hit against the other. Australian Aborigines dance to the rhythm of clashing sticks.

✵ Clay Drum

A Mexican design of the Middle Ages. It comprised two small goblet drums joined by a long hollow clay tube which was bent into a 'U'-shape to bring the two heads into a horizontal line about 60cm (24 inches) apart. One head with an animal skin was beaten by the hands while the other was left open, its tube containing water whose volume could be varied for tuning purposes.

✵ Cymbals

Bronze and other metals are used in non-Western cymbals: two circular plates are clashed together to mark the rhythm. Their distribution is virtually world-wide.

✳ Dai co

In Vietnam this means 'big drum', a large barrel drum with two heads, beaten with sticks.

✳ Da'ira

A tambourine of Mozambique, used to accompany singing. A similar word, *daira*, refers to a Georgian tambourine which may have bells, metal discs and coins round the inside edge.

✳ Da-daiko

A large Japanese barrel drum with two heads each 1.2m (4 feet) in diameter. The instrument is mounted on a heavy wooden frame and played with beaters. The body is 1.5m (5 feet) deep.

✳ Damaran

Paired drums of India, specifically for use in processions and ceremonies. They are conical in shape and hung either side of an ox. The mounted player strikes one drum with a straight stick; the other stick is curved.

✳ Davul

A Near- and Middle-Eastern cylinder drum with two heads, tough laces tensioning the animal-skin heads in a zigzag design. Used in ceremonies and for *al fresco* dancing, the davul of Turkey (*dola* in Kurdish areas) is slung from the shoulder so that both heads may be played, the thicker head uppermost with the heavy beater (*tokmak*), the thinner with a light stick (*cubuk* or *subuk*). Originating in India or Asia about 700 BC, the *davul* now has related instruments in Iran (*dohol*), Armenia (*dool*), Greece (*daouli*) and Albania (*daule*), and is known in Arabia as the 'Turkish drum' (*tabl turki*). The Afghan *dhol* is similar but barrel-shaped and is probably akin to the earliest types since it also survives in India.

✳ Dogdog

A Javanese conical drum with one head.

✳ Doira

A frame drum, sometimes with jingles (thus, a tambourine), played only by women in Afghanistan, Turkey and Iran.

✳ Donno

An hourglass drum (qv) of the *Ashanti* of Ghana.

✳ Drumgong

A Chinese kettledrum dating from the 4th century BC. It is made entirely of bronze, even the single head being of thin bronze, and may be of great size. The head is struck by a heavy beater while the body is played with a bamboo stick to produce a thin, sharp sound.

✳ Dulcimer

A kind of psaltery (see Plucked Instruments) in which the strings are struck with beaters. However, such is the confusion of terms that it is possible to encounter plucked dulcimers and struck psalteries. The terms might thus be regarded as interchangeable.

✳ Fontomfrom

A Ghanaian large drum, similar to the *atumpan*. In common with many non-Western instruments, the name is probably onomatopoeic in origin.

✳ Gamelan

The most important indigenous music of Indonesia, and one of the most eerily evocative to Western ears. Associated today primarily with Bali and Java, *gamelan* orchestras (see panel featuring *gamelan* instruments) seem to have had their origin in a bronze culture that spread from the Asian mainland, not in the form of musical instruments but as weapons of war. Javanese gongsmiths, learning from bronze artifacts left by Asian conquerors, were probably masters of their trade well before the Christian era, and primitive *gamelan* ensembles existed then. Sophistication and evolution then took place and today's *gamelan* ensembles consist of highly organized and superbly disciplined groups of players.

This gong-chime culture developed first in Java, where *gamelan* orchestras were playing by

♩ INDIAN DRUMS AND GONGS BEING PLAYED BY VIRTUOSO UDAY SHANKAR IN 1950.

the 16th century. Balinese *gamelan* ensembles came slightly later and have grown much more diversified in their structure. In addition, west Java and central Java each has its own separate developments. In addition to struck instruments, *gamelan* ensembles can include the *suling*, a long end-blown flute with up to six finger holes; the *rebab*, a local variety of spike fiddle; and singers, either singly or in chorus.

℅ Ganang

A pair of Vietnamese two-headed drums capable of a wide variety of tone: a stick is used upon one head while the hand beats the other.

℅ Ghirbal

A frame drum of Arabia with snares under the single head.

℅ Ghomma

A South African instrument of the Cape Malays: a drum with one head, held under the left arm and played with both palms as an accompaniment to song.

A *GAMELAN* ENSEMBLE, WITH GONG CHIMES, *KENDANG* (CYLINDER DRUM) AND *CHENGCHENG* (CYMBALS) PROMINENT.

℅ Gong

Orchestral gongs (*tam-tams*) evolved from types which take the form of disc-shaped metal plates and are struck centrally or towards the outer edge with beaters of any material (from metal to sponge). Some Eastern gongs have raised central bosses, others have rims. Large gongs are suspended in a frame; this may be of any design because the tone of the gong does not depend upon the frame's shape, see page 32. Gong chimes consist of several tuned gongs set in a stand or framework support that gives the player access to each. See *Gamelan*. The *gong ageng* is a large resonant Balinese gong suspended in a frame. The Japanese *goong* measures in excess of a metre in diameter.

℅ Gourds

Many uses are found for gourds in percussion. In Ghana are floated on water and struck with the palm of the hand or sticks, the water providing resonance. Gourds also provide the bodies of drums and may be filled with pellets to make rattles.

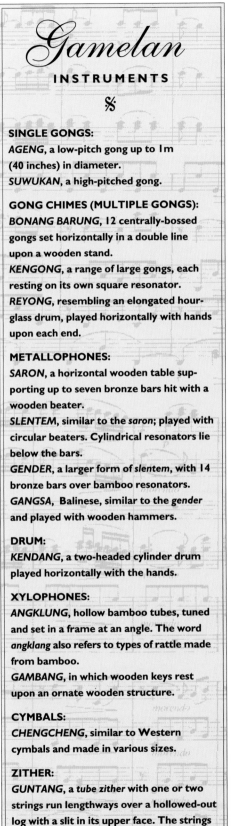

Gamelan
INSTRUMENTS
℅

SINGLE GONGS:
AGENG, a low-pitch gong up to 1m (40 inches) in diameter.
SUWUKAN, a high-pitched gong.

GONG CHIMES (MULTIPLE GONGS):
BONANG BARUNG, 12 centrally-bossed gongs set horizontally in a double line upon a wooden stand.
KENGONG, a range of large gongs, each resting on its own square resonator.
REYONG, resembling an elongated hourglass drum, played horizontally with hands upon each end.

METALLOPHONES:
SARON, a horizontal wooden table supporting up to seven bronze bars hit with a wooden beater.
SLENTEM, similar to the *saron*; played with circular beaters. Cylindrical resonators lie below the bars.
GENDER, a larger form of *slentem*, with 14 bronze bars over bamboo resonators.
GANGSA, Balinese, similar to the *gender* and played with wooden hammers.

DRUM:
KENDANG, a two-headed cylinder drum played horizontally with the hands.

XYLOPHONES:
ANGKLUNG, hollow bamboo tubes, tuned and set in a frame at an angle. The word *angklang* also refers to types of rattle made from bamboo.
GAMBANG, in which wooden keys rest upon an ornate wooden structure.

CYMBALS:
CHENGCHENG, similar to Western cymbals and made in various sizes.

ZITHER:
GUNTANG, a *tube zither* with one or two strings run lengthways over a hollowed-out log with a slit in its upper face. The strings are struck with a short wooden beater.

Types of Drum

The accepted descriptions of drum types clearly indicate their general shape. These descriptions apply equally to non-Western and to orchestral drums.

BARREL DRUM, convex-sided, the body deeper than the diameter of the skin. One or two heads.

CONICAL, its top wider than the base. A double-conical drum resembles two conical drums head to head, with the upper head of a diameter less than that of the waist – a variation of the convex barrel drum.

CYLINDER DRUM, straight-sided, the body of any depth equal to or greater than the diameter of the head. One or two heads.

FRAME DRUM, consisting of a frame of wood or other material, round or square, the diameter of the skin greater than the depth of the body. One or two heads. As with most drums, the design is prehistoric. In Arab countries the generic name for frame drum is *daff, duff, dof,* or something similar. Some Middle Eastern frame drums are adorned with metal jingles round the rim, as in the Western tambourine.

GOBLET DRUM, small, single-headed, with a body tapering to a rounded base, often with a supporting foot.

HOURGLASS DRUM, as if two goblet drums were joined at their bases; therefore, two heads. Some are larger than this description suggests. In India, the hourglass drum has existed for at least 2000 years and survives still. Cords run between the heads and the player exerts pressure on the cords to tighten the skins and thus raise the pitch. In this way, an infinite variety of notes is obtainable within the range of the instrument, and drummers can make the drums 'speak' in a startlingly realistic way. Hourglass drums are also found in Africa.

KETTLEDRUM, bowl-shaped, similar to a goblet drum but larger and more variable in shape.

SLIT-DRUM, primarily an African instrument with a strong tone which may be heard over great distances and is therefore useful as a message drum. Some models are of enormous length, being made from a fallen tree trunk, hollowed out and with slits in the upper surface which vary in size and shape. Edges of the slit form tongues of wood which are beaten with sticks or clubs for dancing or to produce the rhythmic accents of speech for messages. There is no skin membrane.

𝄢 MANY AFRICAN DRUMS DEVIATE IN DETAIL BECAUSE, LIKE THOSE PICTURED, THEY ARE 'HOME-MADE'.

℅ *Gyamadudu*

A cylinder drum of Ghana with two heads. Its name probably derives from its characteristic bass sound, with its slightly muffled initial attack.

℅ *Handle Drum*

A species of African hourglass drum with two heads and a handle carved out from the central body to facilitate manipulation. The presence of the handle precludes the use of tuning ropes. Alternatively, a handle drum may refer to an instrument known from Siberia, through Alaska and into American Indian territory. It is a round frame drum with a handle protruding from it at a tangent. Such a drum is used almost exclusively for religious purposes.

℅ *Harp*

Not usually thought of as a 'banged' instrument, the harp is sometimes called upon to accompany itself with a rhythmic line. In Africa, and inevitably elsewhere, for the temptation must be irresistible, harpists might well add rhythm by playing a tattoo upon the soundboard with their fingers, an intriguing effect caught in Carlos Salzedo's *Chanson de la nuit* (1924) for harp solo.

℁ *Hiuen-ku*

Huge drum of the Chinese Chou dynasty (1122 BC), used in ceremonial events at the Imperial court.

℁ *Hoe*

A simple instrument found in Ghana, consisting of two hoe blades bound together and struck with a metal ring.

℁ *Horns*

In Ghana and other African countries, animal horns are struck with a stick to produce a noise like dull-sounding bells.

℁ *Horseshoes*

An instrument invented by the 18th-century composer John Davy at his blacksmith uncle's workshop. He arranged horseshoes in a given order to produce a melody as they were hit. It is not known whether Davy employed such an instrument in one of his operas.

℁ *Idu-man*

Paired kettledrums of large and small size, found in Tibet.

𝄞 A JAPANESE DRUMMER IN TRADI-TIONAL COSTUME. NOTE THE ANGLED STAND ON WHICH THE DRUM RESTS.

℁ *Isigubu*

Possibly modelled upon European military drums, the *isigubu* was adopted by the Zulus, who modified it with tuning cords attached to the two heads. Playing may be with sticks or hands.

℁ *Ka'eke'eke*

Any hard surface is suitable to make these Hawaiian stamping sticks resound. They are hollowed-out bamboo pipes, usually in sets of four with unequal lengths bound together in pairs, which resonate when 'stamped' vertically on a stone or log. For rhythmic use only.

℁ *Kempul*

A Javanese gong some 50cm (20") in diameter.

℁ *Khong Mon*

A large 'U'-shaped frame, along the inner curve of which are set a series of gongs used in Thai ensembles.

℁ *Khong Wong Yai*

Gongs of Thailand, ranged in a circular rack and struck to make a melody.

℁ *Koboro*

An Ethiopian two-headed drum, sharply angled towards its lower end so that it resembles a kettledrum in appearance. The lower head, therefore, is of much smaller diameter than the upper.

℁ *Ko-daiko*

A large (76cm/30in diameter) Japanese barrel drum with two heads. When used in processions, it is suspended from a pole carried by two men, the player walking alongside striking the instrument with sticks.

℁ *Ko-tsuzumi*

An hourglass drum of Japan, used in *Noh* plays. Cords join the heads and a tuning strap at the central point between the heads. The player holds the instrument against his right shoulder.

℁ *Mpingtintoa*

An onomatopoeic name for a single-headed gourd drum of Ghana.

❦ Mrdangam

A two-headed drum played by both hands horizontally while resting in the player's lap. The word comes from Sanskrit for 'clay-body' (*mrd-anga*), which tells us the material from which the barrel-shaped body is made. The clay, however, is not visible for it is completely coated with cane in a criss-cross pattern. Found in Bangladesh, India and Vietnam, the *mrdangam* probably originated in India.

In an article written in the 1950s, Krishna Chaitanya, an authority on Indian drums, gave an alternative description of the *mrdangam*. He wrote "[It] is hollowed out of a block of wood. A flour paste applied to the left membrane lowers the tone to a full, bass sound while a mixture of manganese dust, iron filings and other substances applied to the right side yields a characteristic resonant tone."

❦ Musical Bow

The bushmen of southern Africa play a hunting bow, one end of which is placed in or near the mouth which acts as a resonator. The string is then struck with a small stick or the fingers while the note is altered by the fingers of the hand holding the bow.

❦ Naqqara

Kettledrums of different sizes found in Arab countries. The name gave rise to the European medieval *nakers*

❦ Ngoma

A large drum, about one metre in diameter, either suspended from a frame or stood on the ground. It has one head and is struck with wooden sticks by women. At South African native ceremonies and important festivals it forms the bass of a drum trio, the tenor drum (*thungwa*) being similar in shape, design and beaters, the alto drum (*murumba*) being small enough to hold between the knees (or stood on the ground on its sturdy single foot) and beaten with the hands.

❦ Nihbash

A domestic pestle and mortar taken from Jordanian kitchens to make a semi-musical rhythm.

❦ Ntenga

A set of tuned drums of Uganda. Each has two heads, the lower one being of much smaller diameter than the upper. With entirely different pitches from each head, and in the usual ensemble of 15 drums, the variety of tone is considerable.

❦ O-daiko

A double-headed 'great drum' of Japanese percussion ensembles, the *o-daiko* barrel drum can measure 2m (6.5 feet) in diameter and weigh over 300kg (660 pounds). It is usually sited permanently on a wooden wagon and requires the services of two drummers, one at each head, who strike the skins with heavy clubs. Forming the rhythmic foundation of the ensemble, the fearsome sound of the *o-daiko* is often accompanied by the warlike shouts of the players

❦ Paakuru

A Maori mouth resonator, consisting of a stick about 40cm (16 inches) long and 1cm thick, shaped like a bow. With one end between the teeth and the other held between two fingers, the player would attack the *paakuru* with a stick and alter the resonance by moving his lips.

❦ Pantaleon

A dulcimer with 185 strings, invented by the German composer from whom it took its name: Pantaleon Hebenstreit. He called it *cimbal*, but Louis XIV insisted in 1705 that the device should carry its inventor's name. In essence, a dulcimer is a horizontal box of strings, these being struck by hand-held beaters. Its popularity survives in the Hungarian *cimbalom*, but in the 18th century it ran somewhat out of control, for in 1767 a pantaleon was made that was no less than 3.35m (11 feet) long, with 276 strings.

♪ A BUSHMAN OF SOUTHERN AFRICA PLAYING A MUSICAL BOW — THE STRIKING ACTION OF THE RIGHT-HAND FINGERS IS AKIN TO PLUCKING.

A SENEGALESE DRUMMER PICTURED IN 1958 PLAYING A BARREL DRUM BY HAND AND STICK.

Pit Xylophone

A Ghanaian instrument consisting of up to 17 wooden keys arranged on a wooden frame, then placed over a resonating pit dug in the earth.

Pit Zither

Occasionally encountered in African communities, the *pit zither* is simply a string or wire held taut by two sticks driven into the ground at the

AN ESKIMO WITH A *QILAIN*, A SINGLE-HEADED FRAME DRUM OF THE TYPE FOUND THROUGHOUT THE ARCTIC ESKIMO COMMUNITIES.

ends of a pit. The player hits the wire with sticks to accompany himself in song.

P'yonjong

A Korean bell-chime in which a wooden frame supports a series of 16 tuned bronze bells struck with a cow-horn mallet.

Qilain

A frame drum of the Eskimo peoples, with a head made of seal skin or the lining of a bear's stomach. The *qilain* differs from other frame drums in being struck with a bone beater only on the rim. The membrane provides resonance as an accompaniment to the Eskimos' most important musical activity: singing, as a social and ceremonial adjunct, often with communities performing against each other in contests.

Beaters

FINGERNAIL For a light touch.

FINGERS Capable of playing fast intricate rhythms.

HANDS The flat of the hand or the heal, thumbs or knuckles, or the fists, may all be used in certain circumstances.

RUBBER Used by West Indian drummers on their steel drums.

LEATHER THONGS For a dull, indefinite attack.

BRUSHES Dance bands often employ the swishing sound of brushes on drum skins.

RODS Wooden rods, for a light but incisive touch.

DRUMSTICKS May be of any size depending upon what drum is being used and the type of sound required. Their heads may be made of anything from the softness of sponge to the hardness of wood; each, of course, producing a different effect. In shape they may range from short to long, straight to sharply curved, and even double-curved. Some short sticks are double-headed, as in Irish folk bands.

BIRCH TWIGS: For the occasional orchestral requirement; they produce a sound rather more incisive than brushes.

BEATERS A word used for any striker, but normally reserved for heavy clubs such as those used in Japanese drumming.

METAL BEATER Used on orchestral tubular bells, and on some instruments of non-Western origin. For instance, metal rings are used on types of fixed bells and on the body of *didjeridoos* while the player is blowing.

Reyong

A Balinese gong-chime, with several gongs ranged in a straight line in a wooden frame and struck by up to four players with hard beaters.

Ringing Stones

Ch'ing. A Chinese instrument dating from the Chou dynasty (up to 221 BC) consisting of an ornate frame upon which hang tuned slabs of stone with were struck by small mallets. In shape the stones recall the side view of a tiger's head.

THE CHINESE *CH'ING*, THE ANCESTOR OF MODERN TUBULAR BELLS. ON THIS EXAMPLE A SMALL BARREL DRUM IS ATTACHED TO THE LEFT-HAND UPRIGHT.

Another example of ringing stones is the *p'yon'-gyong.* Like the linguistically almost identical Korean metal *p'yonjong,* this comprises a wooden framework supporting 16 struck 'bells', but in this case the bells are made of tuned stones rectangular in shape.

Rooria

A Maori Jew's harp made from vegetable fibres up to 10cm (4 inches) long. One end is held between the teeth. Adept practitioners have a way of conversing with one another using their voices and the varying tones of the *rooria.*

Saron

A Javanese trough metallophone. The trough is a long wooden construction upon which is set the *saron.* Like xylophones, metallophones have a system of bars or keys, but of metal, which, when struck in the right order, produce a melody. In the *saron,* the keys are thick and resonate with a deep, rich sound in the trough.

Shield

An unlikely choice as a music-maker, but people from Asia to Africa place them with their convex surfaces to the ground and hit them with beaters, thereby resonating the air trapped underneath.

Shime-daiko

A Japanese barrel drum of small size which serves as much as a physical work-out as an instrument. Its body is hollowed out from a log and the two heads are tensioned by two men who sit facing each other on the floor, the drum held between their bare feet. Great effort is required to tighten the ropes with hands and hammers, the drummers often sweating profusely even before the drums are ready for playing.

Stamping Stick

A hollow drumstick produces resonance. This idea was put to use by primitive peoples, who would beat the stick on the ground or a rock to make a rhythmic accompaniment for dancing. The *ka'eke'eke,* above, is a slightly more sophisticated version of stamping stick.

Steel Drum

In Trinidad, where oil drums were plentiful, workers would cut them in half, divide the head into several tuned sections by cutting and welding, and beat the head with rubber beaters. Steel drum bands make a most acceptable sound, both rhythmically and melodically, and a recording exists of a complete performance of Mozart's *Eine kleine Nachtmusik* played entirely on steel drums.

Stone Star

African tribes enjoy the sound of the stone star. It consists of a circle of stones set in the ground. In the middle sits the player, who strikes the stones, each of which has its own note, with a stone held in each hand.

Sunuj

Arabian finger cymbals, used by dancers. The plates are very small. One, attached to a middle finger, is struck by its fellow on the thumb to make a delicate, high-pitched sound as an accompaniment to dancing and singing.

Tabla

An Indian double drum, used as rhythmic accompaniment in *ragas* and often played alone. The skill of an expert *tabla* player is such that the instrument seems to talk. The upper of the two drums is called the *tabla*; the lower is the *bayan.* The player sits cross-legged with the drums held in the angles of his knees and plays the drums with his hands, using fingertips, flat hands, heels of the hands and sometimes even knuckles and fingernails to produce varied sounds. The tone and pitch varies

THE SKILL AND RHYTHMIC SPIRIT WITH WHICH STEEL DRUMMERS PLAY THEIR INSTRUMENTS HAVE MADE THEIR MUSIC POPULAR WORLD-WIDE.

Heads
AND OTHER STRUCK MATERIALS
℁

SKIN Originally animal skin, dried and stretched taut over a frame.

BARK Tree-bark, suitable for large drums; in some cases the bark was strong enough to support stamping feet.

PLASTIC Modern materials are routinely used in today's drums, being less ecologically unfriendly, stronger, more reliable and cheaper than animal skins.

STRING In the so-called string-drum, a taut string is hit by a stick. In the piano, strings are struck by felt-covered hammers.

WOOD In the slit drum, tongues of wood or the edges of the slits, are struck with beaters. Bamboo strips, cut to tuned lengths are played like a xylophone.

METAL Many non-Western instruments bear metal plates which are struck. Horseshoes are also used. The Trinidad steel drum (see page 38) is made from oil drums cut to size and modified. Anvils are struck with a metal hammer.

VELLUM Used in some smaller drums.

STONE Some rocks resonate when struck.

according to whether the strikes occur on the centre of the head or towards the outer edge.

℁ Tabor

A generic word for 'drum', but more specifically a small cylinder drum slung by a cord round the neck of a pipe and tabor player, who would strike the drum with a stick in one hand while fingering a pipe with the other. *Tabor* also means a long narrow drum, with or without snares, sometimes used in the orchestra.

℁ Tijeras

Bolivian natives used to dance to the rhythm of the *tijeras*: a pair of scissors struck with a hard object to make a sharp sound.

℁ Twenesin

Signal drums of the *Ashanti* peoples, Ghana.

℁ Yamstick

One needs to stand well clear of a *yamstick* player at an Aboriginal totemic corroboree in Australia, for the 'instrument' is merely a stick which is used to beat out the time for the wild dancers, and any object, vegetable, mineral or animal, might serve as a 'drum'.

℁ Zarb

A single-headed goblet drum of the Middle Eastern regions, Iran and the Persian Gulf predominantly but also found in Turkey. It is held under the left arm and played with the fingers of the right hand. A great variety of tones is obtained, depending upon the strength of strikes

and the area of head upon which they are made. Several names attach to the instrument, including *darabukka*, but the Turkish word *dombak* or *tombok* eloquently illustrates the tonal variety of the instrument, from the deep and resonant *tom* to the much shallower, sharper, *bok*.

℁ Zirbaghali

A single-headed goblet drum of Afghanistan, played with the fingers.

THE
Mexican Connection

❊

In his *Xochipilli-Macuilxochitl* ('An Imagined Aztec Music', 1940) the Mexican composer Carlos Chávez assembled a wind group (piccolo, two flutes, E flat clarinet, trombone) and six percussionists to play instruments originating from the time before Columbus. The percussionists' roles were divided as follows:

1. SMALL *TEPONAXTLI*
   OMICHICAHUAZLTI

2. LARGE *TEPONAXTLI*
   SMALL COPPER RATTLES

3. SMALL AND MEDIUM INDIAN DRUMS
   CLAY RATTLE

4. SMALL *HUEHUETL*
   SMOOTH RATTLE

5. MEDIUM *HUEHUETL*
   CLAY RATTLE

6. LARGE *HUEHUETL*
   OMICHICAHUAXTLI

The copper and clay rattles are self-descriptive; a 'smooth rattle' equates with the sound of maracas, a rhythmic swishing of small beans or pebbles in an egg-shaped pod on a stick. The other instruments call for explanation.

ABOVE: A SOUTH AMERICAN NATIVE PLAYING A GOURD MARIMBA.

BELOW: DESCENDANTS OF DANCING AZTECS PICTURED IN 1721, TWO CENTURIES AFTER CORTÉS CONQUERED THEIR LAND AND TWO CENTURIES BEFORE CHÁVEZ ATTEMPTED TO RECONSTRUCT THEIR MUSIC.

GLOSSARY

HUEHUETL A cylinder drum some 90cm (3 feet) tall, standing upon three stout legs contiguous with the body. During construction, the interior is charged with live coals and the animal skin (jaguar or deer) fitted, the heat from the coals drying the skin to a high tension. The outer surface of a *huehuetl* is carved with representations of bird-gods and scenes of war, ritual and revenge.

INDIAN DRUMS These are goblet hand drums of the *bongo* (see page 30) variety.

OMICHICAHUAXTLI A scraper made of bone or wood with notches along one face that are rubbed rhythmically with another bone or stick.

TEPONAXTLI. A two-keyed slit drum (the Mayas called it *tunkul*, and it was known as *tun* in El Salvador). A tree log about one metre long is hollowed, laid horizontally, and an 'H'-shaped slit is cut in the upper surface, the bar of the 'H' at right-angles to the grain of the wood. This gives two keys or tongues of wood which are tuned to give notes a major second or a minor third apart when struck with mallets. Early explorers reported that the 'doleful' boom of the '*teponaxtli*' carried over great distances

All these Aztec instruments found uses in both dance and sacred situations, and Chávez conveyed this in his short composition. However, requirements for its performance are such that normally constituted orchestras cannot mount it without the assistance of museums or collectors.

BANGED ODDITIES

❧ Chinzumana

A xylophone of Mozambique of complicated design. It forms the lowest-sounding in a group of xylophones, its four slats providing a resonant drone. The wooden slats have to be fire-hardened before fitting. Each has a tuned res-onator of wild orange shell, with a hole in the side for a membrane which produces a grating sound. This sound is modified by a wooden pipe leading out from the membrane.

❧ Clapper (or Monkey) Drum

A small double-headed drum from the body of which protrudes a handle. Attached to the body are two short cords, each with a bead, button, pebble or nut secured at the end. When the instrument is twisted rapidly by the handle, the loose objects on cords strike the heads of the drum. The instrument was used by organ-grinders' monkeys to attract crowds; similar versions are found in cultures as remote from Western cities as India, Tibet and Vietnam, which suggests that the *monkey drum*, like its player, originated in the Far East.

❧ Ingpongpo

This *Bantu* drum has a 'head' but no body. A dried animal skin is either manually held off the ground or suspended from poles or tree branches while it is beaten with a stick. The noise, similar to beating a carpet, is useful only as a dancing rhythm or for calling home a foraging party.

❧ Intambula

In Swaziland, south-west Africa, this instrument consists of a clay pot and an animal skin that has been shaved and moistened. These two compo-nents are not attached, and in performance the skin is held tightly in place over the pot by helpers while the player hits it with a stick.

❧ Lithophone

The word means 'stone-sound'. Lithophones take different forms. A standing rock may resound when struck, and in some areas a rock suspended from a rope serves as a bell. Ranges of stones, either suspended or resting upon a frame or the ground (see *Stone star*) are found from China to England; their music resembles that of a series of bells or a xylophone.

❧ Ma-ch'un

An hourglass drum of Tibet, its body being two human skulls joined at the crowns and shaped to take playing skins.

❧ Pahuu

The only *Maori* 'drum' was merely a plank of wood up to 9m (30 feet) in length that was sus-pended from a wooden framework or between two trees. It was a signalling instrument to be beaten by a watchman at times of danger, and it is reported to have been audible up to 20 kilo-metres (12 miles) away. In some models, a hole was pierced at a central point, possibly to give added resonance. 𝄡

𝄞 THE MONKEY DRUM IS VERY EASILY SOUNDED (BY TWISTING THE HAN-DLE) AND EQUALLY USEFUL AS A TOY OR NOISE-MAKER AT FAIRGROUNDS.

𝄞 MISCELLANEOUS & TYPES

SOME INSTRUMENTS SIMPLY do not fit comfortably into any of the categories that we have covered so far in this section. Instead, they exist close to one or more of the standard types, having been invented or discovered under unusual conditions.

❧ *Aeolian Harp*

An instrument of beautiful tone that requires no intervention from humanity to make it sound. There are several different versions, but the most familiar consists of a rectangular frame across which several strings are stretched. All are tuned identically. The instrument is then stood where Aeolus, the wind god, can get at it: a breeze

vibrates the strings and a soft hum fills the area. As the wind increases in strength overtones begin to be drawn from the strings to produce a ghostly, disembodied sound, and if the wind strength or direction change the notes alter in subtle ways. One may imagine the ancients, hearing wind in the reed beds, experimenting with simple constructions of reeds and wooden frames in an attempt to bring the eerie sounds into their domestic environment.

Prehistoric models have been found, and King David is supposed to have owned an Aeolian harp. Much more recently, in the 19th century, experimenters tried to control the instrument by tuning the strings to a scale and constructing a keyboard which operated shutters that would open to allow the wind to reach selected strings. This seems to be unwarranted interference with a charmingly self-sufficient instrument.

❧ *Bull-roarer*

A basic instrument of peoples the world over, but normally associated today with the Aboriginal tribes of northern Australia. It requires little skill and no musical knowledge to make a bull-roarer. A flat piece of wood a minimum of 15cm (6 inches) in length (the maximum length depends upon practicalities, as will be seen) is smoothed,

𝄞 AN AEOLIAN HARP OF ABOUT 1870, MORE SOPHISTICATED IN DESIGN THAN THE EARLIEST EXAMPLES, WHICH WERE PROBABLY CREATED ACCI-DENTALLY BY NATURE.

the edges bevelled and curved, then tapered in both planes at each end. Serrations are added to one long edge. A hole is drilled near one end to take a strong cord. Those bull-roarer makers of artistic bent may feel inclined to carve designs on the flat surfaces. The bull-roarer is also found among Eskimo peoples, where it is fashioned out of bone (fish, seal or bear) or driftwood.

To play the bull-roarer, the cord is gripped at the loose end and the player finds a convenient space. He then whirls it round his head to produce a loud fluttering roar. *Hummer-buzzer, swish, thunderstick* and *bummer* are some of the names the instrument has attracted. The ancients used this mysterious 'sound from nowhere' to scare away women not entitled to attend ceremonies, to stampede cattle and to draw down magic powers from the skies. It is the voice of dead ancestors, they thought. It may also have been used as a weapon, particularly if made from a material other than wood. Stone, bone and iron have all been used. Perhaps, during some forgotten battle, warriors were reduced to hurling flat wooden boards at their enemy and noticed, as the weapons fell, they spun in the air and produced a deep roar. By pitching a short lath into the air, this strange may be demonstrated. That may have spurred the more imaginative among them to make purpose-built roarers.

To add ethnic verisimilitude to his ballet *Corroboree* (1946), the Australian composer John Antill added a bull-roarer to the orchestra. The American Henry Cowell scored his *Ensemble* (1924) for the possibly unique combination of two violins, viola, two cellos and three thunder-sticks.

℅ *Chinese Pavilion*

An inappropriately exotic name for the bell-tree or 'jingling johnny', which is said to have originated as a visible symbol in Turkish military bands as they accompanied their armies to war. Therefore, its alternative name, Turkish crescent, is more appropriate. It consists of a long vertical pole hung with button bells and small cup bells fixed to crescent-shaped cross pieces placed like ladder-rungs. Other decorations, such as plumes, horse tails and patriotic and Islamic emblems

also adorned the instrument. On the march, it rose proud of the soldiers' heads and the carrier would shake it, twist it and bounce it at his feet to accentuate the rhythm of the march.

These military bands included triangles and bass drums since at least the 16th century and

ARM POWER WAS NEEDED FOR THE CHINESE PAVILION BEFORE THE INTRODUCTION OF A HANDLE AND RATCHET DEVICE TO SHAKE THE BELLS.

their sound struck terror into the populations being invaded by the Turks. Mozart, in his opera *Die Entführung aus dem Serail* (1782), Haydn in his Symphony No. 100, 'Military' (1794), and Beethoven in his Symphony No. 9, 'Choral' (1823), are said to have intended the Turkish crescent to be used, but that part is almost invariably taken by triangle, the real thing hardly to be expected as part of a modern orchestra's equipment. Berlioz called for four of them (*pavillon chinois*) in his *Symphonie funèbre et triomphale* (1840).

℁ Handbells

Today we take this term to mean bells which have been graded in size and pitch and played by a 'circle' or 'choir' of players, each responsible for two or four bells. In ancient China, perhaps as much as two millennia before Christ, small bells existed, but there is no evidence that 'circles' of players were organized. Rather, the bells would have been attached to a frame for striking by one or two players. (This use is mentioned under Banged Instruments; it may have contributed to the evolution of the Far Eastern *gamelan* ensembles, see page 33.)

Handbells today are usually shaken by a handle (though occasionally they are lightly struck) and therefore are a species of rattle which, instead of having many loose objects inside, has one captive clapper that swings against the inside of the body when the bell is shaken. Well disciplined circles of players, their bells resting on a covered table before them when not in use, can perform arrangements of most music with considerable skill. It has been essentially an English art since the 17th century but groups of handbell ringers are now active in other countries, particularly in North America.

THE CHINESE ART OF HANDBELL RINGING HAS LARGELY DIED OUT. THIS ILLUSTRATION OF A GROUP OF CEREMONIAL PLAYERS DATES FROM 1846.

℁ Hydraulis

In Greek, *hydro* + *aulos* = water-pipe, though it is really a water-organ. Its invention can be put at 246 BC, when Ctesibius, an Alexandrian engineer who achieved fame for his inventions of the crossbow and the pneumatic catapult, constructed this complicated musical instrument. He took a water tank, a cistern, an air chest, bellows and a set of pipes and arranged them in such a way that a keyboard could produce a tune. A submerged bell in the water tank contained both air and water, the air being supplied by the bellows. A balance was struck between pressure and weight to ensure a steady supply of air to the air chest and thence to the pipes.

Hardly a portable instrument, or a cheap one, the *hydraulis* nevertheless attracted some worthies, and three centuries after it was invented a model so fascinated Emperor Nero that it distracted him from more important matters – such as how to meet an imminent attack from the Gauls. His military staff were instead regaled with a detailed description of the workings of Nero's new *hydraulis*.

℁ Koororohuu

A simple child's toy of the New Zealand Maori. A disc-shaped piece of thin wood or other suitable material is threaded with string through two holes near the centre. By swinging the toy with a circular motion to 'wind it up', then pulling the two ends of the string, a whirring noise is created. Evidence suggests that such toys are by no means restricted to New Zealand.

℁ Lyra Organizzata

This seems to have been an Italian invention of the 1780s or earlier. It was a hurdy-gurdy to which had been added a system of pipes, and the keys of the hurdy-gurdy also controlled the airflow to the pipes. Like the hurdy-gurdy, a handle turned the circular bow under the strings and the player's left hand operated the keys. It is not easy to imagine the sound such a hybrid instrument produced, but when the King of Naples ordered some concertos for two *lyrae organizzate* from Joseph Haydn in 1786,

AN EGYPTIAN *SISTRUM* FROM THE 8TH CENTURY BC. THIS TYPE OF RATTLE EXISTED IN MANY DIFFERENT DESIGNS, OFTEN WITH A FIGURINE ON THE FRAME.

The common football rattle is a ratchet device in which wooden tongues are sprung and released by a cogwheel as the rattle is whirled. The tongues in older examples are sometimes of metal, for such rattles were used as bird scares and as warnings of flood, attack, or fire: their voice had to be heard over wide areas. William Walton called for a wooden rattle, or ratchet, in his *Façade* Suite (1926), and the toy version was used in Leopold Mozart's *Cassatio* in G (1765), parts of which have been popularized as the 'Toy Symphony'.

Wind-chimes

Like the Aeolian harp, wind-chimes are played by the wind. They consist of bells of various sizes which are hung outside or in a window from a frame by cords of different lengths, and allowed to make contact with each other as they swing in the breeze. A charming instrument of no musical value, its gentle sounds are said to calm even the most frayed of nerves.

he instructed that the composer should regard the instrument as sounding like an oboe, but with extremely limited tonal possibilities. As well as Haydn, Ignaz Pleyel, a Haydn pupil, and Joseph Sterkel wrote for the instrument, but their works are lost. Pleyel, much given to rearranging his own music, possibly recycled his for other instruments; Sterkel may have done the same for his instrument, the piano.

Rattle

A rattle is a percussion instrument which is not always 'banged', so could not find a place in the appropriate section above. Any device with hard, loose components, either within a closed vessel or attached outside a frame of some kind, may be regarded as a rattle. The hard pellets might be beads, beans, pebbles, stones, seeds (whole dried seed pods sometimes serve), or buttons. The vessel might be of wood, ceramic, basketwork,

A NIGERIAN PLAQUE DATING PROBABLY FROM THE LATE 17TH CENTURY SHOWING A CHIEF WITH AN ATTENDANT HOLDING A CALABASH RATTLE.

metal, gourd, plastic or any other hard substance. The egg-shaped *maracas* familiar in Latin American bands are of prehistoric origin and wide distribution, and they may be 'banged' on occasion. In his 'Jeremiah' Symphony, (1942) for instance, Leonard Bernstein has them banged against a drum. Dance band percussionists will hit them into the palm of the hand to emphasize a rhythm. In so-called 'external' rattles, the pebbles, teeth, bells, or whatever, are attached to a frame which might take the form of a rigid wooden or metal structure of virtually any shape, or a strap to be shaken rhythmically. The ancient Egyptian *sistrum* consisted of a frame of metal with a handle; within the frame were several cross-pieces along which slid metal disc jingles which struck the frame as the *sistrum* was shaken.

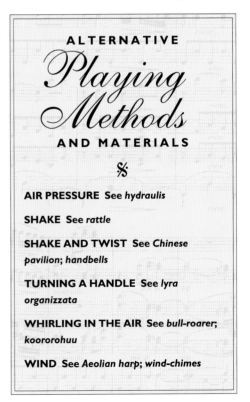

ALTERNATIVE

Playing Methods

AND MATERIALS

AIR PRESSURE See *hydraulis*

SHAKE See *rattle*

SHAKE AND TWIST See *Chinese pavilion; handbells*

TURNING A HANDLE See *lyra organizzata*

WHIRLING IN THE AIR See *bull-roarer; koororohuu*

WIND See *Aeolian harp; wind-chimes*

INDEX
NON-WESTERN & OBSOLETE INSTRUMENTS

Non-Western and Obsolete Instruments

The publishers would like to thank the following sources for their kind
permission to reproduce the pictures in this book:

AKG London, Ancient Art & Architecture Collection, Bonani, Jean-Loup
Charmet, Corbis, Mary Evans Picture Library, Werner Forman Archive,
Maureen Gavin Picture Library, Michael Holford, Hulton Getty, Performing
Arts Library/Steve Gillett, Popperfoto, University of Edinburgh/Collection of
Historic Musical Instruments

Every effort has been made to acknowledge correctly and contact the source
and/or copyright holder of each picture, and Carlton Books Limited
apologises for any unintentional errors or omissions which will be corrected in
future editions of this book.

About the Author

Robert Dearling is a respected classical music writer and reviewer. In addition to being a specialist in the music of the 18th century, he has considerable knowledge of musical instruments and over the past 30 years has amassed a huge database of information pertaining to the histories and uses of the world's instruments. He has a wide knowledge of music journalism and has written for many periodicals. He has also written over 400 sleeve and CD booklet notes for among others, Decca, EMI, RCA and Sony. His books include *The Guinness Book of Music*, *The Guinness Book of Recorded Sound*, and *Mozart – The Symphonies*.